BEI GRIN MACHT SICH WISSEN BEZAHLT

- Wir veröffentlichen Ihre Hausarbeit,
  Bachelor- und Masterarbeit

- Ihr eigenes eBook und Buch -
  weltweit in allen wichtigen Shops

- Verdienen Sie an jedem Verkauf

Jetzt bei www.GRIN.com hochladen und kostenlos publizieren

Bibliografische Information der Deutschen Nationalbibliothek:

Die Deutsche Bibliothek verzeichnet diese Publikation in der Deutschen National-
bibliografie; detaillierte bibliografische Daten sind im Internet über http://dnb.d-
nb.de/ abrufbar.

Impressum:

Copyright © 2014 GRIN Verlag, Open Publishing GmbH
Druck und Bindung: Books on Demand GmbH, Norderstedt Germany
ISBN: 9783668316072

Dieses Buch bei GRIN:

http://www.grin.com/de/e-book/341062/datenjournalismus-aus-konstruktivistischer-
perspektive

Wilke Bitter

Datenjournalismus aus konstruktivistischer Perspektive

Sind Datenanalysemethoden die Grundlage für eine neue Objektivitäts-Hybris?

GRIN Verlag

Datenjournalismus aus konstruktivistischer Perspektive

Sind Datenanalysemethoden die Grundlage für eine neue Objektivitäts-Hybris?

Bachelorarbeit im Studiengang Medien, Kommunikation, Gesellschaft

Sommersemester 2014

Universität Trier

Vorgelegt von

Wilke Bitter

Studiengang: BA Medien, Kommunikation, Gesellschaft (Hauptfach)

Fachsemester: 6

Inhalt

1 Einleitung

1.1 Datenjournalismus – Mehr als ein Trend?

Einen großen Schub an Aufmerksamkeit bekam die Praxis des Datenjournalismus mit den Geschichten, die laut Simon Rogers, einem der prominentesten Autoren, nur mit Hilfe datenjournalistischer Mittel aus den Datensätzen der „Afghanistan war logs" geschrieben werden konnten, die im Jahr 2010 über die Plattform WikiLeaks veröffentlicht worden waren:[1] „The WikiLeaks releases on Afghanistan, Iraq and the US embassy cables; [...] reporting on all of those events was arguably only possible because of, and was irrevocably changed by, the existence of reporters whoe are not afraid of maths, know how to use a spreadsheet, work with the lates web visualization tools and – crucially – know what questions to ask."[2] Die Onlineformate der New York Times und des Guardian bereiteten, für die Nutzer interaktiv zugänglich, zehntausende Dokumente auf.[3]

Julian Assange, Mitbegründer der WikiLeaks-Plattform, sah die neuartige Berichterstattung als eine notwendige Entwicklung des Journalismus in Richtung Wissenschaftlichkeit: „I want to set up a new standard: 'scientific journalism.' If you publish a paper on DNA, you are required, by all the good biological journals, to submit the data that has informed your research – the idea being that people will replicate it, check it, verify it. So this is something that needs to be done for journalism as well. There is an immediate power imbalance, in that readers are unable to verify what they are being told, and that leads to abuse."[4]

Heute, so die Vertreter und Beförderer datenbasierten Berichtens, sei Datenjournalismus im Mainstream des Journalismus angekommen. „Ninety years later, publishing those sacred facts has become a new type of journalism in itself: Data Journalism. And it's rapidly becoming part of the establishment."[5] Da Datenjournalismus ohne in ausreichender, periodisch erstellter Menge der namensgebenden Daten unmöglich ist, spielen Initiativen von Staaten und Kommunen, ihre Regierungsgeschäfte offenzulegen, und die Arbeit von Datenaktivisten wie der „Free our Data movement" des Guardian eine große Rolle in der Verbreitung des Datenjournalismus.[6] Gleichzeitig wächst zudem die Anzahl der

---

[1] Vgl. Rogers (2013): S. 43 und S. 78.
[2] Ebd.: S. 30.
[3] Vgl. Beckedahl (2011).
[4] Khatchadourian (2010).
[5] Rogers (2013): S. 10.
[6] Ebd.: S. 33.

„Leakingplattformen" wie WikiLeaks, auf denen zumeist geheime Regierungsdokumente der Öffentlichkeit zugänglich gemacht werden.[7]

Journalistenschulen wie die Poynter News University nutzen das Interesse an journalistischer Datenverarbeitung und richten zahlreiche Kurse ein, um dem Bedürfnis vieler Journalisten, mit dem Trend mitzuhalten, gerecht zu werden.[8] Gleichzeitig allerdings, so Guardian-Chefredakteur Alan Rusbridger, weichten kostenlos verfügbare Mittel zum Berichten die traditionelle Funktionsteilung in der Gesellschaft zwischen Produzenten und Rezipienten auf, die heutige „Kommunikationsrevolution" der Digitalisierung und Verarbeitung von großen Mengen von Daten sei vergleichbar mit der Erfindung des Buchdrucks und habe ein „Zersplittern" des Journalismus als vierte Gewalt in der Gesellschaft zur Folge.[9]

Für die publizistikwissenschaftliche Betrachtung der Produzenten in dieser neuen Dynamik, der Journalisten, sind besonders die Haltungen und Ansichten, Motive und Beweggründe zur Adoption grundsätzlich neuer Wege der Berichterstattung interessant. Die vorliegende Arbeit wirft in diesem Zusammenhang ein Schlaglicht auf die ideologischen Hintergründe von Datenjournalisten. Unter der Fragestellung „Beeinflussen die Methoden des Datenjournalismus das Selbstbild von Journalisten in dem Sinne, dass sie an objektivere Berichterstattung glauben?" wird in der Arbeit untersucht, inwiefern Datenjournalisten eine Art Überzeugung teilen, mit sich wissenschaftlichen Standards annähernden Erhebungsmethoden einen besseren Zugriff auf eine in sich subjektunabhängige Realität zu haben. Die wissenschaftliche Beantwortung der Fragestellung kann nach Faulstich am ehesten der Publizistikwissenschaft zugeordnet werden, da sie den Fokus der Arbeit auf die Pragmatik im Journalismus im Sinne einer Instanzenforschung richtet.[10]

In quantitativen Befragungen von Journalisten wies ein Großteil der Befragten eine Affinität zu realistischen Konzepten von Wirklichkeit auf: Zwar sei es schwierig, so die häufigsten Antworten, aber dennoch möglich und für die Qualität journalistische Produkte ausschlaggebend, durch den gewissenhaften Vergleich von medienexterner und abgebildeter Realität Berichterstattung möglichst wirklichkeitsnah zu leisten.[11]

---

[7] Vgl. Beckedahl (2011).
[8] Quelle: Homepage der Poynter News University (URL:
https://www.newsu.org/search/node/data%20journalism [Abgerufen: 08.09.2014]).
[9] Vgl. Rusbridger (2010).
[10] Vgl. Faulstich (2004): S. 183 und Faulstich (2004): S. 187.
[11] Vgl. Pörksen (2006): S. 25.

Letztlich befindet Simon Rogers, dass Datenjournalismus das Geschäftsmodell Journalismus auf lange Sicht bewahren kann: „It represents a new role for journalists as a bridge and guide between those in power who have the data (and are rubbish at explaining it) and the public who desperately want to understand the data and access it but need help.“[12]

Der deutsche Onlinejournalismus, im Speziellen der Spiegel Online, scheint nach Lorenz Matzat hinterhergehinkt zu haben. Der fehlende Mut der Verlage und Redaktionen zum Testen neuer Formate und die im Vergleich zu den Vereinigten Staaten von Amerika dünn besiedelte Stiftungslandschaft für Journalismus seien als Ursachen hierfür zu nennen.[13]

Eine prägnante und kurze Definition für den Begriff Datenjournalismus zu finden ist eine Herausforderung: Die vielen unterschiedlichen, unübersichtlichen Aspekte dieser journalistischen Praxis machen einen kurzen Umriss schwer. Zu unterscheiden ist Datenjournalismus jedoch in jedem Fall von Computer Assisted Reporting, einer seit mindestens zwei Jahrzehnten gebräuchlichen Methode: CAR, bei dem ein Computer beispielsweise Rechercheassistenz leistet, ist heutzutage in jeder Spielweise des Journalismus anzutreffen, daher nicht synonym mit Datenjournalismus zu nennen.[14]

Eine Gemeinsamkeit der Definitionen des Datenjournalismus ist indes die Dreiteilung der Praxis in Recherche- und Datenverarbeitungsmethoden sowie neuartige Erzählweisen. Troy Thibodeauxs Definition befasst sich mit dem ersten Punkt: „Real data journalism comes down to a couple of predilections: a tendency to look for what is categorizable, quantifiable and comparable in any news topic and a conviction that technology, properly applied to these aspects, can tell us something about the story that is both worth knowing and unknowable in any other way.“[15]

Simon Rogers, Pionier der digitalen, datenverarbeitenden Berichterstattung beim britischen Guardian, erweitert die Rechercheinnovation durch die neuen Möglichkeiten, Geschichten zu erzählen: „If data journalism is about anything, it's the flexibility to search for new ways of storytelling.“ [16] Paul Bradshaw, Journalistentrainer bei selbiger Zeitung, betont die Gleichgewichtung der drei Aspekte des Datenjournalismus: „It represents the convergence of

---

[12] Rogers (2013): S. 43.
[13] Vgl. Beckedahl (2011).
[14] Vgl. Thibodeaux (2011) und Beckedahl (2011).
[15] Thibodeaux (2011).
[16] Rogers (2013): S. 22.

a number of fields which are significant in their own right – from investigative research and statistics to design and programming."[17]

Nach Lorenz Matzat umfasst der Begriff in seiner griffigen, deutschen Defintion „[...] eine Kombination aus einem Recherche-Ansatz und einer Veröffentlichungsform: Ein oder mehrere maschinenlesbare Datensätze werden per Software miteinander verschränkt und analysiert – damit wird ein schlüssiger und vorher nicht ersichtlicher informativer Mehrwert gewonnen. Diese Information wird in statischen oder interaktiven Visualisierungen angeboten und mit Erläuterungen zum Kontext, Angaben zur Datenquelle (bestenfalls wird der Datensatz mit veröffentlicht) versehen."[18]

1.2 Stand der Forschung

Die Redaktionsforschung des Pew Research Center befindet, dass während große Nachrichtenunternehmen wie Time Inc. Und Tribune Co. Jobs abbauen, derzeit immer mehr hochqualifizierte, prämierte Journalisten von kleineren, an sozialen Medien orientierten und große Mengen von Daten verarbeitenden Online-Portalen („digital native news") wie Mashable.com oder BuzzFeed abgeworben werden.[19]

Ein wachsendes Bedürfnis nach der Interpretation der in der heutigen Welt permanent und allseits gesammelten Daten macht es für professionelle Journalisten wie für Blogger attraktiv, sich mit Datenaufbereitung und –analysen auseinander zu setzen.[20] Die Fähigkeiten für die Suche und gewinnbringende Analyse von großen Datenmengen sollten sich nach Ansicht von Hochschuldidaktikern angehende Journalisten in einer revidierten Journalistenausbildung aneignen können.[21]

„Policies" von staatlichen Regierungen, Administrationsdaten generell der Öffentlichkeit zugänglich zu machen, werden in der Literatur für den Datenjournalismus als hilfreich erachtet. [22] Diejenigen Redaktionen, die für den Bereich des Datenjournalismus mit ausreichend Mitteln ausgestattet sind, unterhalten ein „Datenjournalismus-Team", in dem die unterschiedlichen Bereich von Zugang und Aufbereitung der Daten, der Analyse, Interpretation und Projektmanagement arbeitsteilig organisiert sind.[23]

---

[17] Vgl. Bradshaw (2010).
[18] Dietrich (2010).
[19] Vgl. Pew Research Center (2014): S. 2f.
[20] Vgl. Meckel/Fieseler/Grubenmann (2012): S. 8.
[21] Vgl. Ebd.
[22] Vgl. Ebd.: S. 9.
[23] Vgl. Ebd.

Zum größten Teil kostenlos online verfügbare Werkzeuge („tools") wie Google Fusion Tables stehen Journalisten aber auch außerhalb solcher Teams zur Verfügung, um Datensätze zu sortieren und Anwendungsmöglichkeiten zu schaffen. [24] Das Bedürfnis moderner Redaktionen, Datenjournalismus mit möglichst niedrigen Personalkosten zu betreiben, stellt angehende und praktizierende Journalisten vor die attraktive Option, sich dem Datenjournalismus zu nähern. [25]

Die Medienphilosophin Mercedes Bunz bewertet den Datenjournalismus als bedeutende Umwälzung von Wissensprozessen im Journalismus. Die Digitalisierung erfasse den Journalismus als Vorreiter informationsverarbeitender Berufsfelder als erstes und womöglich mit den größten Auswirkungen: Die Miniaturisierung von Informationen habe eine bahnbrechende Beschleunigung von Wissensprozessen zur Folge, die sich in elementarem Sinne auf Berichterstattung auswirken wird. [26] In einem sich wissenschaftlicher Vorgehensweisen annäherndem Journalismus ist das Testen der Datenquellen auf ihre Verlässlichkeit und der Ausbau journalistischer Transparenz durch die Einführung von Belegen für die Stichhaltigkeit von Behauptungen in Veröffentlichungen notwendig. [27] Letztlich lasse sich die politische Funktion der Journalisten, Geheimnisse über Missstände aufzudecken, nur anhand von authentischen Quellen realisieren. [28]

Die Wahl der theoretischen Perspektive der Arbeit fiel aufgrund der Auseinandersetzung mit Objektivitäts- und Wirklichkeitsbegriffen auf den Konstruktivismus in Medien- und kommunikationswissenschaftlicher Spielweise. Theoriegeleitete Erkenntnisbestrebungen sind in der qualitativen Forschung eher selten anzutreffen, in einer Arbeit wie der vorliegenden kann eine Theorieperspektive jedoch durchaus nützlich in der Bildung der forschungsstrukturierenden Hypothesen sein. [29]

Aus der Perspektive des „diskursiven Konstruktivismus" Bernhard Pörksens werden im Anschluss an die Diskussion der verwendeten empirischen Erhebungsmethode in der vorliegenden Arbeit, des Experteninterviews mit anschließender Textinterpretation, der konstruktivistische Diskurs in der Medien- und Kommunikationswissenschaft kurz umrissen und die forschungsstrukturierenden Hypothesen vorgestellt, die auf Überlegungen auf der Basis des „diskursiven Konstruktivismus" aufgestellt werden.

---

[24] Vgl Meckel/Fieseler/Grubenmann (2012): S. 9.
[25] Vgl. Ebd.: S. 10.
[26] Vgl. Bunz (2011).
[27] Vgl. Ebd.
[28] Vgl. Ebd.
[29] Vgl. Gläser/Laudel (2010): S. 31.

Die von den hier interviewten Datenjournalisten vertretenen Haltungen werden im daran anschließenden Kapitel zusammengetragen und im Analyseteil dem geisteswissenschaftlichen Verstehensprozess, strukturiert durch konstruktivistische Überlegungen, unterzogen.[30]

2 Methodendiskussion

2.1 Das Experteninterview

Die empirische Befragungsmethode des Leitfadeninterviews, in der Arbeit in der Form des Experteninterviews verwendet, besteht aus am Erkenntnisziel orientierten und in ihrer Reihenfolge strategisch gegliederten Fragen an ein Gegenüber, deren explizite Formulierung erst im Interview mit einem ausgewählten Experten eine feste Form findet.[31] Der Verzicht dieser Methode auf explizite, leitende Regeln macht indes eine genaue Dokumentation der Vorgehensweise notwendig. Geeignet ist diese Art der Befragung laut Literatur zur Rekonstruktion und anschließenden geistes- oder sozialwissenschaftlichen Erklärung von sozialen Prozessen und der Untersuchung von Ansichten und Motiven.[32]

Die bis auf die Reihenfolge der Fragen und die erwünschten Wechselwirkungen zwischen den Fragen nicht weiter festgelegten Leitfadeninterviews profitieren der Methodenliteratur zufolge von ihrer Offenheit: Spontane Zwischen- und Verständnisfragen und die erwünscht ausführlichen und detaillierten Antworten der Gesprächspartner sind hier möglich, da kein vorgegebenes Antwort- oder Frageschema verwendet wird.[33]

Um den „Fluss" des Interviews und damit seine der natürlichen Kommunikation eines Gesprächs angenäherte Form zu verbessern und dem Erkenntnisinteresse zuträgliches Nachfragen zu ermöglichen, ist seitens des Interviewers eine gewisse Vertrautheit mit dem Forschungsgegenstand vorausgesetzt.[34]

Gleichzeitig aber lässt sich über das Interview mit einem Experten auch ein Zugang zu einem fremden Feld mit vergleichsweise günstiger Forschungsökonomie in puncto Aufwand schaffen: [35] Die Dichte der Informationsgewinnung und die häufig anzutreffende Auskunftsbereitschaft von Experten macht die Methode des Leitfadeninterviews in jenen Forschungszusammenhängen in der Kommunikations- und Medienwissenschaft zu einer

---

[30] Vgl. Gläser/Laudel (2010): S. 37.
[31] Vgl. Pürer (2003): S. 540 und Faulstich (2004): S. 189.
[32] Vgl. Gläser/Laudel (2010): S. 13.
[33] Vgl. Pürer (2003): S. 540.
[34] Vgl. Ebd.: S. 541.
[35] Vgl. Bogner/Littig/Menz (2009): S. 8f.

beliebten Wahl, deren Ziel nicht repräsentative Erhebungen, sondern die genaue Aufzeichnung einer Fülle von Details ist. Besonders geeignet ist diese Methode daher auch laut Pürer für Explorations- und Pilotstudien.[36]

In einem erfolgreich etablierten Gesprächsfluss soll der Charakter des Interviews einer wissenschaftlichen Erhebung allmählich verschwinden. Die in anderen Forschungsmethoden der Erhebung vorgeschaltete Operationalisierung von Begriffen geschieht nach Gläser/Laudel durch den „natürlichen" Gesprächscharakter des Interviews „on the fly": Während des Interviews bewältigt der Interviewer anhand des im Vorfeld erstellten Leitfadens, der theoretische Vorüberlegungen widerspiegelt, eine „permanente, spontane Operationalisierung".[37] Der Gültigkeit, der Validität der Methode kommt dies nach Pürer zu Gute, da sich die Aussagen der Gesprächspartner weniger dem sozial Erwünschten, sondern eher ihren tatsächlichen Meinungen und Ansichten annähern, die sie in anderen Kontexten, in denen sie nicht die Rolle einer wissenschaftlich genutzten Quelle von Informationen spielen, ebenfalls vertreten würden.[38]

Durch den über das Forschungsobjekt gut informierten Interviewer, der ein Gespräch in die Richtung eines bestimmten Erkenntnisinteresses leitet und mit gesprächsfördernden, (para-) sprachlichen Äußerungen in Gang hält, wird der Eindruck erweckt, es bei den Experteninterviews mit einer für Reaktivität besonders anfälligen Erhebungsmethode zu tun zu haben.[39] Nach Bernhard Pörksen ist dies aus konstruktivistischer Sicht bei Befragungen aller Art unausweichlich: „Den Beobachter vermag man nicht einfach, nur weil dies programmatisch gefordert wird, aus dem Erkenntnisprozess herauskürzen; er stellt auch in strikt standardisierten Forschungsprozessen unvermeidlich jene Größe dar, die sich nicht eliminieren lässt."[40]

Andererseits sorge eine persönliche Involviertheit in die Erhebung für Authentizität der Ergebnisse und eine leichtere Rekonstruktion der Selbstbetrachtung des Gegenübers.[41]

Der Frage, inwiefern sich die Methoden von dem Problem der Reaktivität befreien lassen oder von ihren geistes- und sozialwissenschaftlichen, erkenntnistheoretischen Wurzeln trennen lassen, wird hier nicht nachgegangen. Stattdessen hält sich die Arbeit an die Ansicht Siegfried

---

[36] Vgl. Pürer (2003): S. 540.
[37] Vgl. Gläser/Laudel (2010): S. 112 und S. 115.
[38] Vgl. Pürer (2003): S. 541 und Gläser/Laudel (2010): S. 113.
[39] Vgl. Gläser/Laudel (2010): S. 112.
[40] Pörksen (2006): S. 107.
[41] Vgl. Pörksen (2006): S. 112.

J. Schmidts, dass für konstruktivistische Forschung einerseits keine neue Methodologie von Nöten ist, besondere Sorgfalt allerdings der kritischer Reflexion der verwendeten Methoden, der forschereigenen Epistemologie und der Ergebnisse am Ende des Forschungsprozesses gelten muss.[42]

2.1.1 Auswahl der Interviewpartner

Die Auswahl der Interviewpartner wurde unter Berücksichtigung der von Gläser und Laudel aufgestellten Kategorien getroffen, die eine erfolgreiche Erhebung mittels Experteninterview zum Zweck eines bestimmten Erkenntnisgewinns sichern sollen:[43] Zunächst sorgten die Aspekte der Verfügbarkeit bzw. der Gesprächs- und Informationsbereitschaft für eine quasi automatische Vorauswahl. Anschließend wurden aus den verbleibenden, gesprächsbereiten Experten jene ausgewählt, deren Expertise unter Berücksichtigung der Ergebnissicherung durch die Triangulation verschiedener Quellen dem Erkenntnisgewinn zuträglich eingeschätzt wurde. Letztlich wurde die Anzahl der Interviews aus forschungsökonomischen Gründen auf zwei Expertengespräche begrenzt.[44]

2.1.2 Erstellung des Fragebogens

Die Erstellung des Leitfadens für die Experteninterviews und die vorläufige Formulierung der erst im Gespräch explizit formulierten Fragen wurde einerseits anhand der theoriegeleiteten Annäherung an das empirische Forschungsfeld und der daraus hervorgegangenen Hypothesen und andererseits anhand der vier Funktionsdimensionen nach Gläser und Laudel erarbeitet:

Aus inhaltlicher Hinsicht wurden erstens sowohl Faktfragen, die Erfahrungen und Hintergrundwissen beleuchten sollen, als auch Meinungsfragen verwendet, die eher auf die Motive, Wertvorstellungen und Ziele des Gegenüber abzielen.[45]

Gegenstandbezogene Fragen sollen zweitens den Gesprächspartner mit hypothetischen Forschungsvermutungen konfrontieren, sprachlich gestaltet allerdings möglichst ohne das Forschungsinteresse permanent sichtbar zu machen.[46]

Drittens wurde mit der Formulierung der Leitfragen auf die angestrebte Gestaltung der Antworten in der Form von zu Erzählungen im Detail motivierenden Fragen abgezielt.[47] Mit „Ja" oder „Nein" zu beantwortende Fragen wurden dazu gezielt vermieden. Durch das

---

[42] Vgl. Pörksen (2006): S. 109.
[43] Vgl. Gläser/Laudel (2010): S. 117.
[44] Vgl. Ebd.: S. 118.
[45] Vgl. Ebd.: S. 123.
[46] Vgl. Ebd.: S. 123.
[47] Vgl. Ebd.: S. 124 und S. 132.

tatsächlich sehr hohe Mitteilungsbedürfnis der Interviewpartner wäre die Erhebung allerdings in der Rückschau auch an kurzen Fragen vermutlich nicht gescheitert.

Schließlich wurden die Leitfragen viertens in einer spezifischen Reihenfolge geordnet und in einer bestimmten Weise umformuliert, die einer Gesprächsführungsstrategie wie Einleitungs-, Überleitungs-, Irritations-, und Hauptfragen zur Erhebung gemäß dem Erkenntnisinteresse dienen.[48]

Der den Interviews zugrunde liegende Leitfaden wurde auf die ausgewählten Interviewpartner angepasst, ohne jedoch eine gewisse Vergleichbarkeit der Aussagen zu gefährden: Nachdem klar wurde, welche Interviewpartner zur Verfügung stehen, wurden die Fragebogen zunächst im Vorfeld um einige wenige Frageaspekte zur sozialen und professionellen Umwelt der Gesprächsgegenüber angepasst und während der Gespräche weiterhin via „Einstellen auf den Gesprächspartner" und „Aktives Zuhören" individualisiert.[49]

2.1.3 Analyse der Aussagen

Die Auswertung und Analyse der Experteninterviews in dieser Arbeit basiert in Grundzügen auf der qualitativen Inhaltsanalyse nach Gläser und Laudel. Aus forschungsökonomischen Beweggründen wurde diese Methode jedoch in ihrem Umfang für die Arbeit angepasst: Mithilfe eines in der theoriegeleiteten Untersuchung des Forschungsfeldes angepassten Suchrasters werden relevante Äußerungen in offener, nicht weiter dokumentierter Weise kodiert, um dann in freier Interpretation analysiert zu werden.[50] Das offene Kategoriensystem des Suchrasters ermöglicht die Untersuchung von Merkmalsausprägungen ohne Codes und Skalen im Vorfeld festlegen zu müssen und erlaubt, komplexe Zusammenhänge verstehend zu bearbeiten.[51]

Auf „manifeste" Inhalte der Kommunikation in einer Inhaltsanalyse abzuheben, wäre aus der für die Arbeit gewählten konstruktivistischen Perspektive aufgrund einer nicht anzunehmenden singulären Bedeutung von Text inkonsistent:[52] Letztlich sollen statt objektiver Fakten Ansichten unter Berücksichtigung deren Kontingenz interpretiert, nicht abgebildet werden.[53]

---

[48] Vgl. Gläser/Laudel (2010): S. 127 und S. 145.
[49] Vgl. Ebd.: S. 117, S. 150, S. 173 und S. 178.
[50] Vgl. Ebd.: S. 200f.
[51] Vgl. Ebd.: S. 200.
[52] Vgl. Pörksen (2006): S. 111.
[53] Vgl. Ebd.: S. 118.

3 Konstruktivismus als forschungsstrukturierende Theorieperspektive

3.1 Spielarten des Konstruktivismus: Gemeinsame Denkfiguren

Unter dem Begriff Konstruktivismus lässt sich nach Siegfried J. Schmidt im Allgemeinen weder ein festes Theoriegebäude noch eine Gruppe von Wissenschaftlern mit homogenen Ansichten zusammenfassen, sondern vielmehr ein gemeinsamer Diskurs unterschiedlicher Wissenschaftsdisziplinen, die die erkenntnistheoretischen Prämissen in puncto Realismus und objektiver Erkenntnis ihrer eigenen Forschungstraditionen in Frage stellen.[54]

Bernhard Pörksen fasst sein Verständnis von Konstruktivismus pragmatisch zusammen, denn hier „[…] wird der Wechsel der Perspektiven und Beobachtungsweisen als ein Denkstil vorgeschlagen, der dabei hilft, so genannte Gewissheiten, letzte Wahrheiten, große und kleine Ideologien so lange zu drehen und zu wenden, bis sie unscharfe Ränder bekommen - und man mehr sieht als zuvor."[55]

Vertreter des Konstruktivismus nehmen nach Pörksen damit die schwierige Position zwischen Anhängern des Realismus, die bewusstseinsunabhängige, höchstens zu entschleiernde ontische Realität und Wahrheit für gegeben halten, und dem Solipsismus, deren Vertreter Postulate formulieren, die Beweise der Existenz der bewusstseinsunabhängigen Außenwelt ablehnen.[56]

Zu den Gemeinsamkeiten der unterschiedlichen Wissenschaftsdisziplinen, deren Heimat unter anderem biologisch-naturwissenschaftliche, psychologische, kybernetische oder wissenssoziologische Forschungstraditionen sind und die konstruktivistische Zweige ausgebildet haben, gehören Themen wie die Betrachtung von Beobachtungen, Strukturdeterminiertheit und Systemtheorien und das Ziel, die als prozessual verstandene Entstehung von wahrgenommener Wirklichkeit zu beobachten und herauszuarbeiten.[57]

Ihr „kleinster gemeinsamer Nenner" in puncto Konstruktivismus lässt sich nach Schmidt wie folgt formulieren: In einer kognitiv-sozial definierten Welt werden individuelle Operationen und deren Bedingungen relevant: Statt mit „Was"-Fragen nach den Objekten der Prozesse

---

[54] Vgl. Schmidt (1994): S. 4 und Pörksen (2006): S. 27.
[55] Pörksen (2006): S. 9.
[56] Vgl. Ebd.: S. 27.
[57] Vgl. Schmidt (1994): S. 4 und Pörksen (2006): S. 28.

werden „Wie"-Fragen fruchtbringend bei der Suche nach Rückschlüssen, anhand welcher Elemente die Konstruktion sozialer Wirklichkeit geschieht.[58]

Als Vertreter einer Theorie oder vielmehr Denkschule der Beobachtung zweiter Ordnung, d.h. als Beobachter von Beobachtern, Akteuren und Kommunizierenden, bemühen sich Konstruktivisten um die Analyse und Interpretation dieser zwar willkürlichen, aber oftmals gesetzmäßigen Wirklichkeitskonstruktion anhand des Prinzips der Beobachterrelativität:[59] „Jede Erkenntnis ist nur eine Beobachtung und ist relativ zu den Kategorien eines bestimmten Beobachters."[60]

Die Erstellung solcher Kategorien ist für das Subjekt schlicht notwendig, da es die Wirklichkeit, ob man ihre Existenz nun abstreitet oder befürwortet, aus konstruktivistischer Sicht nicht in Gänze verarbeiten kann. Die Unterscheidungsoperationen allerdings, die für das Aufstellen der Wahrnehmungskategorien vorgenommen werden müssen, weisen eine Bewertung der einen Reizelemente als relevant, anderer Elemente als weniger relevant auf:[61] Notwendigerweise wird nun der großer Teil der „Restwelt" ausgeblendet und der, etwas euphemistisch betitelte, „blinde Fleck" der Wahrnehmung entsteht.[62]

Die Betrachtung der Wahl dieser Kategorien und den darin enthaltenen, bewussten oder unbewussten Unterscheidungen von wahrgenommen Elementen der Realität, die letztlich für die Beimessung von Bedeutung durch das Subjekt relevant sind, lässt aus konstruktivistischer Sicht Rückschlüsse auf die individuellen Wahrnehmungsoperationen eines Subjekts zu. Jene Unterscheidungen beruhen also auf individuellen Bewertungen von Relevanz und haben zur Folge, dass manche Reize in den Vordergrund der Wahrnehmung rücken und andere nicht. Physisch und psychisch limitiert kann ein Subjekt nicht die Realität, ob es sie nun gibt oder nicht, in ihrer Gänze verarbeiten.[63]

Bernhard Pörksen betont in diesem Zusammenhang den pragmatischen Nützlichkeitscharakter des Konstruktivismus für jedwede wissenschaftliche Forschung als „produktive Heuristik": Die Unzugänglichkeit oder Non-Existenz einer ontologisch subjektunabhängigen Realität hält konstruktivistische Forscher nicht notwendigerweise davon ab, statt dem Wesen von Dingen das Entstehen von sozialen und kognitiven Wirklichkeitskonstruktionen und deren

---

[58] Vgl. Schmidt (1994): S. 5.
[59] Vgl. Schmidt (1994): S. 5.
[60] Pörksen (2006): S. 39.
[61] Vgl. Ebd.: S. 40.
[62] Vgl. Ebd.: S. 40f.
[63] Vgl. Ebd.

Bedingungen zu untersuchen. [64] Konstruktivistische Konzepte sollen in einem „Anregungsverhältnis" zwischen dem Erkenntnisinteresse und der durchgeführten Untersuchung stehen.[65]

Der Radikale Konstruktivismus nach Ernst von Glasersfeld, dessen Anhänger in dem Konzept einen Paradigmenwechsel für alle Wissenschaftszweige vermuteten, indes schließt mit dem Ziel der Untersuchung von Voraussetzungen und Mechanismen kognitiver und kommunikativer Wirklichkeitskonstruktion an eine alte philosophische Auseinandersetzungstradition an: Die zentrale Stellung des Subjektes in seiner individuellen Erlebniswelt bedingt die Existenz von so vielen Realitäten, wie es Subjekte gibt. [66] Konstruktivisten sehen in diesem Zusammenhang ihre Aufgabe darin, den Eindruck, in einer gemeinsamen Wirklichkeit zu leben, zu untersuchen.[67]

Aus dem den Denkstil widerspiegelnden Schreibstil der Konstruktivisten soll im Idealfall, so Bernhard Pörksen, der Charakter des Denkansatzes als „eye-opener"[68] also zur grundsätzlich neuen Wahrnehmung befähigender Denkschule hervorgehen. Der Konstruktivismus soll in der Forschung keine neuen, allgemeingültigen Paradigmen und Vorannahmen installieren sondern in der Akzeptanz der Beobachterabhängigkeit jeder Erkenntnis die Formulierung von flexiblen, offenen, bearbeitbaren Thesen ermöglichen.[69]

Im Allgemeinen wird, so Glasersfeld und Pörksen, ein (individueller, journalistischer) objektiver Zugriff auf, oder sogar das bloße Vorhandensein der Realität in Frage gestellt, da die selbstreferenziell wahrnehmenden Individuen nur innerhalb ihrer ganz eigenen Unterscheidung zur Außenwelt die Möglichkeit zur sicheren Erkenntnis haben.[70] Der Begriff der Selbstreferenzialität stammt aus der Hirnforschung: „Die Kriterien für Bedeutungshaftes entstammen vielmehr stets dem System selbst, auch wenn sie bei individuellem Lernen oder im Laufe der Evolution in Auseinandersetzung mit der Umwelt gewonnen werden. Dies ist die grundsätzliche Selbstreferenzialität […] des kognitiven Systems."[71]

---

[64] Vgl. Ebd.: S. 38.
[65] Vgl. Scholl (2011): S: 445 und Pörksen (2006): S. 67.
[66] Vgl. Schmidt (1994): S. 6 und Pörksen (2006): S. 37.
[67] Vgl. Schmidt (1994): S. 10
[68] Vgl. Pörksen (2006): S. 22.
[69] Vgl. Ebd.: S. 22.
[70] Vgl. Schmidt (1994): S. 7f.
[71] Ebd.: S. 9.

3.2 Konstruktivismus in der Medien- und Kommunikationswissenschaft

3.2.1 Diskursgeschichte

Die Idee, eine vom Subjekt unabhängige Realität anzuzweifeln und daraus einen Skeptizismus gegenüber Aussagen zu entwickeln, die sich der Wahrheits- und Realitätstreue brüsten, ist aus philosophiegeschichtlicher Sicht keine Neuheit: Schon vorchristliche Skeptiker befassen sich mit dem Subjekt als einzigem sicheren Anhaltspunkt für Erkenntnis. Daraus entwickelt sich eine philosophische Tradition, die sich bis in die Moderne fortsetzt.[72] Allerdings, so Pörksen, kann von einer konstruktivistischen Tradition durch die historisch- und sozio-kulturellen Hintergründe der einzelnen Autoren nicht gesprochen werden, vielmehr lassen sich ähnliche Ansätze unter dem Stichwort des „epochenspezifisch begründeten Skeptizismus" zusammenfassen.[73]

Das Anliegen der Konstruktivisten aus der Forschungstradition der Kommunikations- und Publizistikwissenschaft, besonders Siegfried Weischenbergs, war nach Scholl die Revision der kulturpessimistischen, auf die Verzerrung der Realität abhebenden Journalismusforschung in den 1970er und 1980er Jahren. Die Konstruktionsregeln des Journalismus sollten aufbereitet werden, um Kritik an Einflussfaktoren auf das Berufsfeld wie Arbeitsprozesse, Sozialisation und Ethik üben zu können.[74]

Nachdem Diskussionen um den Radikalen Konstruktivismus Glasersfelds im Funkkolleg „Medien und Kommunikation" 1991/1992 rund um die Jahrestagung der Deutschen Gesellschaft für Publizistik und Kommunikationswissenschaft erhitzt geführt worden sind, betrieben Siegfried Weischenberg und Armin Scholl in der ersten Hälfte der 1990er Jahre Bemühungen, den systemtheoretischen Funktionsaspekt des Subsystem Journalismus auf die Konzepte des Radikalen Konstruktivismus zu übertragen:[75] Durch die Strenge der Beobachterabhängigkeit in den Konzepten der letzteren Denkschule negieren die Autoren so jeglichen Zugriff auf eine objektive Darstellung der Realität im Journalismus. Objektivität wird zur „Wahnvorstellung", Beobachtungen ohne Beobachter machen zu können und von einer berufsbefähigenden Prämisse zur „operativen Fiktion" herabgestuft und, durch in

---

[72] Vgl. Pörksen (2006): S. 30.
[73] Vgl. Scholl (2011): S. 446 und Pörksen (2006): S. 30.
[74] Vgl. Scholl (2011): S: 448.
[75] Vgl. Pörksen (2006): S. 46.

individuellen Realitäten individueller Rezeptionen, Gesetze für Medienrezeptionseffekte für unmöglich erklärt.[76]

3.2.2 Anwendung konstruktivistischer Konzepte in der medien- und Kommunikationswissenschaft

Im Kontext von journalistischer Berichterstattung und der Verwendung von Medien zur Übertragung von Informationen rückt aus konstruktivistischer Sicht die Frage nach der Verlässlichkeit der Wirklichkeitskonstruktionen in den Vordergrund, auf deren Basis die Rezipienten der Medien sich innerhalb der Gesellschaft orientieren.[77] Dieser Frage widmen sich Konstruktivisten in der Medien- und Kommunikationswissenschaft, seitdem Siegfried F. Schmidt diesem Wissenschaftszweig ein theoretisches Gegenstück sozialwissenschaftlicher Forschung zur traditionellen, werkimmanent-heuristischen Literaturtheorie entwarf.[78]

Diejenigen Ansätze des Konstruktivismus, die in den Medien- und Kommunikationswissenschaften hauptsächlich verwendet werden, unterscheiden sich von den naturalistischen Theoriemodellen aus den Naturwissenschaften durch ihre kulturalistische Fokussierung auf soziale Interaktionsorte und -prozesse wie Sprache, Kommunikation, Medien, Kultur und Gesellschaft.[79]

Dadurch, dass Massenmedien in jedem gesellschaftlichen Bereich eine tragende Rolle spielen, gewinnen Fragen nach der Plausibilität von Behauptungen, Bildern und Darstellungen an Gewicht,[80] denn die Wirklichkeit der Produzenten hat maßgeblichen Einfluss auf die transportierte „Realität" in den Medienprodukten.[81]

Besonders zu problematisieren ist hier nach Schmidt erstens der gewohnte Konsum von ähnlichen Produkten, bei dem die Künstlichkeit und Perspektivität der Medienprodukte aus der bewussten Rezeption verschwinden kann. Zweitens, so Schmidt, fördert der zunehmender Abstraktionsgrad oder eine zunehmende Distanz von Medienprodukten zur sinnlichen Wahrnehmung die Komplexität der Konstruktionen und damit deren Intransparenz.[82]

---

[76] Vgl. Pürer (2003): S. 170f und Pörksen (2006): S. 42.
[77] Vgl. Schmidt (1994): S. 12.
[78] Vgl. Scholl (2011): S: 446.
[79] Vgl. Pörksen (1994): S. 29.
[80] Vgl. Schmidt (1994): S. 15f.
[81] Vgl. Ebd.: S. 16.
[82] Vgl. Ebd.: S. 12.

Objektivität wird von einer berufsbefähigenden Prämisse zur „operativen Fiktion" herabgestuft und, durch die Annahme von in individuellen Realitäten individueller Rezeptionen, Effektdetermination von Weischenberg und Schmidt für unmöglich erklärt.[83]

3.2.3 Diskursiver Konstruktivismus: Journalismus- und Wissenschaftskritik

Bernhard Pörksen vertritt die Position, den Ansätzen des Konstruktivismus in der Wissenschaft im Allgemeinen der Hochschullehre der Journalistik im Speziellen eine produktiv-irritierende Funktion einzuräumen, denn:[84] „Offenbar wird die Eigengesetzlichkeit, die Autonomie journalistischer Wirklichkeitskonstruktionen und die zunehmende Relevanz von Medien für die moderne Welterfahrung."[85]

Hierzu fasst er konstruktivistische Theoriepostulate in dem Konzept des diskursiven Konstruktivismus zusammen, den er als „epochenspezifisch begründeten, idealerweise anregender und zu nichts verpflichtender Skeptizismus" verstanden wissen will.[86] Die Feindlichkeit gegenüber Dogmen und einschränkender Perspektivität soll den diskursiven Konstruktivismus auszeichnen, eine notwendige Folge der Selbstanwendung konstruktivistischer Prämissen.[87]

So soll, frei von ideologischen oder objektivitätsbeanspruchenden Fixierungen besonders in dem für pointierte, zielgerichtete Betrachtungen bekannten Berufsfeld des Journalismus die Eigengesetzlichkeit (Autonomie) beziehungsweise die Einseitigkeit von Betrachtungen beobachtet werden können:[88] „Es geht darum, etwas zu beobachten, was eine anderer nicht beobachtet, um ihn auf diese Weise auf blinde Flecke zu sensibilisieren."[89]

Essentieller Bestandteil des diskursiven Konstruktivismus ist die Perspektivfreiheit in Verbindung mit der Abhängigkeit des Konzepts von einem singulären Forschungsobjekt: Dadurch, dass hier keine Prüfkriterien, keine Codes oder Skalen für einen Nachweis eines wie auch immer gearteten Zusammenhangs einer Wirklichkeitskonstruktion vorgegeben sind, muss das Konzept mittels „Viabilitätssuche" auf die jeweils relevanten Forschungsobjekte angepasst werden, da sich die beleuchtende, enthüllende Wirkung des diskursiven

---

[83] Vgl. Pürer (2003): S. 170f.
[84] Vgl Pörksen (2006): S. 13.
[85] Vgl. Ebd.: S. 17.
[86] Vgl. Ebd.: S. 16.
[87] Vgl. Ebd.: S. 63.
[88] Vgl. Ebd.: S. 63.
[89] Ebd.: S. 63.

Konstruktivismus nur in direkter Konfrontation mit dem Objekt des Interesses entfalten kann.[90]

Ein von Pörksen für die Anwendung des diskursiven Konstruktivismus vorgeschlagenes Anwendungsobjekt sind Wissenschaftsdiskurse, denen sich via „wissenschaftskritischer Sensibilisierung" zu nähern ist: In der Betrachtung naturwissenschaftlicher Aussagen und Behauptungen, denen die Verwendung subjektunabhängiger, objektiver Forschungsmethoden zugrunde liegt, kann eine grundsätzliche Skepsis der Perspektiven und Annahmen gegenüber einen Zweifel an Ergebnissen und Postulaten mit Wahrheitsanspruch legitimieren.[91]

3.2.4 Im Fokus: Konstruktivistische Inspiration für das Forschungsfeld Datenjournalismus

Das „spezifische Ad-Hoc-Expertentum" [92] der Journalisten, sich unter Zeitdruck der „Newsroom-Deadlines" in zum Teil höchst komplexe Zusammenhänge einzuarbeiten und diese in verständlicher Weise aufzubereiten beinhaltet oft die gefährliche Notwendigkeit, sich auf Ansichten von Experten oder die Perspektivität bestimmter Quellen verlassen zu müssen. Dabei steigt für die Berichterstattung die Relevanz der Wissenschaft derzeit enorm: Als verlässliche Informationsquelle, aber auch als Vorbild für das Finden und die Darstellung von (statistisch aufbereiteten, visualisierten) methodisch nachgewiesenen Tatsachen, Stil und Sprache beeinflussen wissenschaftliche Diskurse das Tagesgeschäft des Journalismus stark.[93]

Journalismus, und besonders wissenschaftlich betriebenem Journalismus gegenüber ist es nach Pörksen notwendig, sich „ [...] deutungskritischer Reflexionsweisen als einer wissenschaftsadäquaten Methode der Vorurteils- bzw. Hypothesenprüfung" zu bedienen. So sollen von der Wissenschaft aufgestellte und vom (Wissenschafts-)Journalismus verbreitete letztgültige Gewissheiten und wissenschaftliche Wahrheiten erkenntnistheoretisch fundiert in Zweifel gezogen werden. [94] Nach Schmidt sind es die Abstraktionsgrade dieser Art der Berichterstattung, die durch die Distanz zur individuellen Sinneserfahrung eine problematische Intransparenz schaffen. [95] Die Kritik am vertretenen Realismus steht im Vordergrund diskursiv-konstruktivistischer Beobachtungen: Annahmen von

---

[90] Vgl. Ebd.: S. 64.
[91] Vgl. Pörksen (2006): S. 87.
[92] Vgl. Ebd.: S. 90.
[93] Vgl. Ebd.: S. 90ff.
[94] Vgl. Ebd.: S. 93.
[95] Vgl. Schmidt (1994): S. 12.

Beobachterunabhängigkeit in Konzepten der Berichterstattung, besonders in wissenschaftlichen Kontexten, sind zu prüfen.[96]

Für das Vorhaben dieser Arbeit, das Selbstverständnis von Datenjournalisten als wissenschaftlich arbeitende Berichterstatter zu analysieren, hat das Konzept des diskursiven Konstruktivismus einen inspirierenden, anregenden Charakter: Durch die Formulierung der klassischen Kritikpunkte des Konstruktivismus am Realismus, angewandt auf den Bereich des Journalismus, konnte anhand der Ausführungen Pörksens eine erkenntnistheoretisch fundierte Betrachtungsperspektive auf die Aussagen der Datenjournalisten in den Interviews und im medialen Diskurs um diese neue Spielart des Journalismus erarbeitet werden, die das Überprüfen folgende Forschungshypothesen erfordert:

1. Das Selbstbild des subjektiven Betrachters gesellschaftlicher Zusammenhänge verliert im Fall von Datenjournalisten zugunsten des Selbstbildes objektiver "Präsentatoren".

2. Die Nutzung von großen Datensätzen veranlasst Journalisten zu der Annahme, den zwangsläufig vorhandenen "blinden Fleck" journalistischer Berichterstattung verringern zu können.

3. Behauptungen durch Zahlen zu legitimieren, ist der wichtigste Bestandteil datenjournalistischer Praxis.

4. Datenjournalisten vertrauen empirisch-systematisch erhobenen Daten und den sich daraus ergebenden Zusammenhängen.

5. Datenjournalisten vertrauen auch ohne Verständnis für den statistischen Background Werkzeugen, die Sinn aus großen Datenmengen gewinnen können.

6. Scheinbar legitimiert durch die "Wahrheit der Zahlen" inszenieren Datenjournalisten einen neuen, intransparenten Typ von Medienwirklichkeit.

---

[96] Vgl. Pörksen (2006): S. 100.

4 Experteninterviews

4.1 Kurzportraits der Experten

4.1.1 Derek Willis

Derek Willis ist Mitarbeiter als Master of Professional Studies in Journalism der journalistischen Fakultät an der Georgetown University und arbeitet seit 2007 als Web-Entwickler und Beauftragter für die Beschaffung von Daten für die New York Times.[97] Im Segment „Upshot" publiziert er über Kongresswahlen und entwickelt er in enger Zusammenarbeit mit Journalisten Programmierungen, die die Visualisierungen und Interaktivität der onlinejournalistischen Inhalte ermöglichen, deren Geschichten auf der Analyse von großen Mengen von Daten basieren.[98]

4.1.2 Matt Waite

Seit 2007 befasste sich Matt Waite für die St. Petersburg Times mit der Kombinierung seiner journalistischen Erfahrung und der Programmierung von onlinebasierten Anwendungen, die die Visualisierung- und Interaktivität innerhalb von Artikeln ermöglichen.[99] Neben der Web-Entwicklungsfirma Firma Hot Type Consulting gründete er 2007 zusammen mit anderen Journalisten der Tampa Bay Times die mittlerweile mit einem Pulitzer-Preis ausgezeichnete Homepage PolitiFact, die die Aussagen von Politikern durch „Crowdsourcing" auf ihren Wahrheitsgehalt hin prüft.[100] Derzeit unterrichtet Matt Waite als Professor of Practice angehende Journalisten am College of Journalism and Mass Communication der University of Nebraska-Lincoln in der Journalistik und digitaler Produktentwicklung.[101]

---

[97] Quelle: Portrait Derek Willis'; Homepage der Georgetown University und der New York Times. (URL: http://scs.georgetown.edu/departments/11/master-of-professional-studies-in-journalism/faculty-bio.cfm?a=a&fId=173924 [Zugegriffen: 08.09.2014] und http://topics.nytimes.com/top/reference/timestopics/people/w/derek_willis/index.html [Zugegriffen: 08.09.2014]).

[98] Quellen: Derek Willis' Homepage und Interview mit Derek Willis in der Zeitschrift Capital (URL: http://thescoop.org/about/ [Zugegriffen: 08.09.2014]) und http://www.capitalnewyork.com/article/media/2014/08/8550292/60-second-interview-derek-willis-reporter-emtimesem-upshot [Zugegriffen: 08.09.2014]).

[99] Quelle: Matt Waites Seite auf der Homepage der University of Nebraska-Lincoln (URL: http://journalism.unl.edu/waite-matt [Zugegriffen: 08.09.2014]).

[100] Quellen: Matt Waites Seite auf der Homepage der University of Nebraska-Lincoln und die Homepage PoltiFact (URL: http://journalism.unl.edu/waite-matt [Zugegriffen: 08.09.2014] und http://www.politifact.com/about/ [Zugegriffen: 08.09.2014]).

[101] Quelle: Matt Waites Blog (URL: http://blog.mattwaite.com/ [Zugegriffen: 08.09.2014]).

4.2 Zusammenfassung der Experteninterviews

4.2.1 Auseinandersetzung mit Datensätzen: Obligatorisch für Journalisten

Innerhalb des Berufsfeldes des Onlinejournalismus ist den Ansichten der interviewten Experten zufolge die Verpflichtung, sich mit Daten auseinanderzusetzen, nicht zu missachten. Die Menge erhobener verfügbarer Daten steige in der heutigen Welt rasant und die Journalisten müssen darüber und daraus berichten. Falls sie dies nicht oder nur mit Hilfe tun können, seien sie keine guten Journalisten.[102]

Die Notwendigkeit für Reporter, sich mit der Verarbeitung von großen Datenmengen auseinander zu setzen, ergebe sich aus dem beruflichen Bedürfnis, in einer sich wandelnden Umwelt fähig zu bleiben, über die Handlungen von gesellschaftlichen Instanzen wie großen Institutionen und Organisationen berichten zu können und im Wettbewerb mit anderen Journalisten nicht unterzugehen.[103] Die Fähigkeit, mit großen Mengen von Daten umgehen zu können, sei eine derzeit im Geschäft des Journalismus gefragte Eigenschaft eines Journalisten und laut Derek Willis aus individueller, selbstbewahrender Perspektive sehr attraktiv, da sie dem einzelnen Reporter einen Vorteil verschaffen kann.[104]

4.2.2 Datenjournalistische Methoden: Der Nutzen

Datenjournalisten können sich dank ihrer Methoden laut Willis ansonsten unmöglich in der Beantwortung zu realisierenden, gesellschaftlich allerdings relevanten und vielversprechenden Fragestellungen nähern und, dank der definitiven, eindeutigen Logik der Datenauswertung, mit Autorität und Sicherheit auf die eine oder die andere Weise beantworten.[105]

Die Optionen, eine Geschichte zu präsentieren, nehmen laut Matt Waite, Professor of Practice an der University of Nebraska-Lincoln, durch die Methoden des Datenjournalismus zu: Die Zusammenhänge, auf denen die Berichte basieren, können mithilfe von Visualisierungen und Interaktivität den Rezipienten näher gebracht werden.[106]

Die Aussagen Matt Waites und Derek Willis' stimmen in dem Punkt überein, dass mithilfe datenjournalistischer Methoden die Fähigkeiten der Journalisten erweitert werden können, indem die Limitierungen menschlicher Berichterstatter überwunden werden: Nach Waite sind

---

[102] Vgl. Waite: S. 3; Z. 65 – 69.
[103] Vgl. Ebd.: S. 3; Z. 72 – 86.
[104] Vgl. Ebd.: S. 4; Z. 94 – 98 und Waite; S. 3; Z. 83 – 84.
[105] Vgl. Ebd.: S. 4; Z. 92 – 101.
[106] Vgl. Waite: S. 4; Z. 88 – 90.

datenjournalistische Werkzeuge Erweiterungen der menschlichen Fähigkeiten und eine Aufhebung menschlicher Limitierungen, da sie Tag und Nacht anhand von vorher definierten Kriterien der Relevanz Informationen sammeln.[107]

Dadurch, dass auf die Erfassung von bestimmten Stichworten und Parametern in Daten programmierte Computer keine Pause machen müssen und auch sonst keine der menschlichen Bedürfnisse oder Beschränkungen haben, ist die Bandbreite der von Berichterstattung abgedeckten Realität größer als bei der traditionellen Berichterstattung.[108] Diese Erweiterung der Aufnahmefähigkeit und Filterungsmöglichkeiten der Realität sollten vom Journalismus genutzt werden.[109] Dies kann das Konsultieren von Experten nach Derek Willis zwar Experten als in vielen Fällen legitime Tradition im Journalismus nicht ersetzen, vor dem Hintergrund der eigenen Autonomie sollten Journalisten Chancen, die sich bieten, völlig neue Wege der Informationsgenerierung für die Berichterstattung zu finden, unbedingt nutzen.[110]

4.2.3 Journalistische Expertise: Zentral im Datenjournalismus

Letztlich kann die Aufbereitung und Interpretation von Daten jedoch nur eine der vielen wichtigen Fähigkeiten eines Journalisten sein, so Willis:[111] Die Legitimität und die Aussagekraft von Behauptungen, die aufgrund von Daten gemacht werden, sind immer nur so gut, wie die Korrektheit und Fairness der Interpretation der Daten.[112] Blinde Flecken und eine individuelle Sichtweise auf die Realität lassen sich nach Matt Waite auch durch die Verwendung datenjournalistischer Methoden letztlich nicht abschaffen. Das journalistische Talent, im Interview neugierig zu sein und die richtigen Fragen zu stellen, ist auch beim „Interviewen" von Daten ausschlaggebend für Erfolg.[113]

4.2.4 Annäherung an die Wahrheit

Dadurch, dass in den Artikeln mithilfe von auf Daten basierenden Visualisierungs- und Interaktivitätsmodulen ein Überblick über Nachrichtendiskurse gegeben werden kann und große Zusammenhänge über einen großen Zeitraum hinweg beschrieben werden, bekommen die Aussagen in den Artikeln laut Derek Willis eine eindeutige, endgültige Betonung.[114] Eine Berichterstattung, die auf Daten basiert, könne der Annäherung an die tatsächlichen Zusammenhänge von Ereignissen in einer objektiven Wirklichkeit zugutekommen und Muster

---

[107] Vgl. Waite: S. 2; Z. 39-42.
[108] Vgl. Willis: S. 9; Z. 252 – 254.
[109] Vgl. Ebd.: S. 9; Z. 273 – 274.
[110] Vgl. Ebd.: S. 11; Z. 328 – 332.
[111] Vgl. Ebd.: S. 7; Z. 193 – 196.
[112] Vgl. Ebd.: S. 7; Z. 185 – 186.
[113] Vgl. Waite: S. 8; Z. 241 – S. 9; Z. 255.
[114] Vgl. Willis: S. 2; Z. 43 – 57.

von Ereignissen in korrekter Weise aufzeigen.[115] Auch Matt Waite betont: „You'll be able to see the world in more complete and empirical ways. Your stories will have a foundation that is much stronger than they would with, you know, four anecdotes and a bunch of interviews."[116]

Allerdings, so befindet Matt Waite, besteht die Gefahr eines zu großen Vertrauens auf die Aussagen, die aus den in den Daten vorhandenen Zusammenhängen gefunden werden können: "[…] that is this kind of belief that I see on the part of a lot of data journalists that because there is data, it does mean that it is true."[117] Vorsicht sei auch laut Willis in der Praxis des Datenjournalismus vor einer sich schleichend ausbreitenden Gewissheit geboten, einem Glauben an die Allmacht der Daten.[118]

4.2.5 Unbestechliche Computer

Viele angehende Journalisten haben nach Matt Waite Angst vor oder eine Aversion gegen Mathematik. Allerdings ist es das logische Denken der Mathematik, das zur korrekten Verwendungen datenjournalistischer Methoden notwendig ist. [119] In einigen Fällen verwendeten Journalisten Methoden, deren Funktionsweise sie nicht verstehen. Die Katastrophen, die aus solch fahrlässigem Verhalten resultieren können, könnten das Ende einer Karriere bedeuten.[120]

Das Vertrauen auf den unbestechlichen, unzweideutigen Wahrheitscharakter maschinell ermittelter Fakten, das besonders bei Journalisten mit einer Aversion für Mathematik und die Programmierung von Programmen auftrete, könne laut Derek Willis eine Gefahr für stichhaltige Berichterstattung darstellen: „I do think that […] it can seem for some folks, the fact that a computer spits out some number, can seem more authoritative than it otherwise should be and they have this sort of trust in the computer that usually comes from the sense of 'Well, the computer seems smarter than I am.'"[121]

Hinzu kommt eine Blindheit für die potenzielle Einseitigkeit der Berichterstattung auf der Basis von großen Datenmengen, die aus Gewohnheit resultiert: Die Perspektivität der eigenen Betrachtung, auch von scheinbar objektiven Zusammenhängen aus Datensätzen, verschwinde

---

[115] Vgl. Willis: S. 7; Z. 187 – 188.
[116] Waite: S. 3; Z. 85 – S. 4; Z. 87.
[117] Waite: S. 4; Z. 108 – 109.
[118] Vgl. Willis: S. 7; Z. 210 – 211.
[119] Vgl. Waite: S. 10; Z. 280 –285.
[120] Vgl. Ebd.: S. 10; Z. 297 – 301.
[121] Willis: S. 8; Z. 234 – 237.

nach Derek Willis aus der Reflexion der Journalisten, je ausgiebiger und je länger sie mit Datensätzen arbeiten.[122]

4.2.6 Autorität von Daten

Anders als für menschliches Denken unerreichbare wahrhaftige Objektivität könne die wissenschaftliche Stichhaltigkeit datenjournalistischer Berichterstattung laut Waite den Behauptungen und Meinungen von Journalisten eine gewisse Autorität verleihen.[123]

Letztlich stellten diese Methoden nur eine aussagekräftigende Ergänzung des journalistischen Werkzeugkastens dar,[124] wissenschaftliche Aussagen zu treffen sei nicht das Ziel von Journalisten: „[…] and I'm not sure I would want us to start shooting fort he pursuit of scientific truths in some respects."[125] So schränkt auch Willis den prinzipiellen Wahrheitscharakter auf Daten basierender Aussagen ein. Er betont, dass immer dort Vorsicht geboten ist, wo die Repräsentativität der Aussagen durch die Daten eingeschränkt ist. Aus einem spezifischen Kontext gewonnene Daten sind nicht in der Lage, Aussagen in einem anderen Kontext zu erklären.[126] Datensätze müssten wie Interviewpartner einem „Background-Check" unterzogen werden: Die Daten müssen in ihrer Herkunft, Konsistenz und Repräsentativität in Bezug auf den betrachteten Zusammenhang stimmig sein, bevor Behauptungen auf ihrer Grundlagen gemacht werden könnten.[127]

4.2.7 Methodologische Transparenz: Notwendigkeit und Motive der Unterlassung

Um Trugschlüssen vorzubeugen, plädiert Matt Waite für mehr Transparenz und Kompromisslosigkeit in der Anwendung der Methoden im Datenjournalismus: Methodologische, wissenschaftlichen Standards genügende Strenge bei Verarbeitung von Daten für die Berichterstattung könne das Ansehen von berichterstattenden Medien verbessern.[128] Diese, wenn auch unter dem Zeitdruck der Redaktionen limitierte Weg wissenschaftlich-reflexiver Vorgehensweise, die kritischer Betrachtung standhält, sei für diese Art des Journalismus prinzipiell unerlässlich.[129]

Obwohl es kein großer Bestandteil journalistischer Praxistradition ist, so Derek Willis, wäre die Transparenz über die Gewinnung der in Artikeln verbreiteten Informationen eine

---

[122] Vgl. Willis: S. 5; Z. 124 – 129.
[123] Vgl. Waite: S. 7; Z. 202 – 211.
[124] Vgl. Willis: S. 8; Z. 214 – 215.
[125] Vgl. Ebd.: S. 8; Z. 219 – 220.
[126] Vgl. Ebd.: S. 4; Z. 112 – 120.
[127] Vgl. Ebd.:S. 5; Z. 129 – 130.
[128] Vgl. Waite: S. 6; Z. 166 – 169.
[129] Vgl. Waite: S. 6; Z. 178 – S. 7; Z. 188.

notwendige Ergänzung datenjournalistischer Produkte. Von allzu großer Vertrauenswürdigkeit der eigenen Methoden auszugehen und seine Ergebnisse dementsprechend zu vermarkten, sei gefährlich.[130]

Unter Datenjournalisten, besonders unter denen, die in angesehenen Medienhäusern angestellt sind, werden laut Derek Willis die Bemühungen um Transparenz über die eigenen Methoden immer beliebter. Allerdings sollte seiner Meinung nach die Transparenz nicht gesondert stehen von den Aussagen der Geschichten: „[…] but honestly i think the better part is to put it right in the story and say: 'Look, here's what we don't know about this. Here's the weakness of this data.'"[131] Letztlich werden die Leser im Zeitalter des Internets früher oder später herausfinden, ob die Berichterstattung eines Anbieters vertrauenswürdig ist oder nicht.[132]

In diesem Zusammenhang stelle die Öffnung des Berufsfeldes des Journalismus durch das Internet einen bedenklichen Aspekt dar: Der Trend zum Datenjournalismus und der Wettbewerb um die Selbstprofilierung bedingt, dass eine große Menge Menschen ohne Erfahrung mit Fehlschlägen und daraus resultierendem mangelnden professionellen Skeptizismus zum Journalismus kommen.[133]

In einer Rangliste der Gründe, warum Journalisten, im Speziellen Datenjournalisten ihr Arbeitsweisen nicht präzise offenlegen, steht nach Matt Waite der Zeitdruck an erster, Faulheit an zweiter und die Verweigerung, sich mit möglichen methodologischen Unstimmigkeiten in der eigenen Arbeit auseinanderzusetzen, an dritter Stelle.[134] Letztlich würde methodische Transparenz sich für die einzelnen Reporter nicht auszahlen: „I think there are news agencies that rather spend time on the story and not creating some kind of methodological explanation."[135]

4.2.8 Die Leser werden Transparenz fordern

Sowohl Matt Waite als auch Derek Willis vertreten die klassisch-liberalistische These, dass zu kritisierende Mängel in der Qualität der Berichterstattung durch fehlende methodologische Transparenz letztlich vom „Markt" nicht auf lange Sicht geduldet werden: Früher oder später wird das Publikum nach Derek Willis im Internet mehr Transparenz bezüglich der

---

[130] Vgl. Willis: S. 5; Z. 147 – S. 6; Z. 152.
[131] Ebd.: S. 6; Z. 165 – 166.
[132] Vgl. Willis: S. 6; Z. 174 – 179.
[133] Vgl. Waite: S. 5; Z. 136 – 138 und Waite; S. 6; Z. 156 – 157.
[134] Vgl. Ebd.: S. 13; Z. 394 - 398.
[135] Ebd.: S. 13; Z. 378 – 379.

verwendeten Methoden verlangen, denn Ausreden wie der im Printjournalismus fehlende Platz für die Erklärungen der Vorgehensweisen haben hier ihre Gültigkeit verloren.[136] Ebenso Matt Waite: „The marketplace will […] see non-serious, non-rigorous journalism, they will be duped by stories and they will ultimately feel put off by that and they will respond to it by no longer going to that news organization and then that news organization will cease to exist."[137]

5 Problematisierung des Datenjournalismus aus konstruktivistischer Perspektive: Test der Hypothesen anhand der Experteninterviews

Untersucht wurde in den Experteninterviews, ob das Selbstbild von Journalisten sich durch die Verwendung datenjournalistischer Methoden wandelt, von einem subjektiven Betrachter gesellschaftlicher Ereignisse zum Kurator von Daten; zum objektiven, durch die Wissenschaftlichkeit seiner Analysemethoden von jeglichem „Bias" befreiten „Präsentator".

Tatsächlich glaubt den Aussagen Derek Willis zufolge eine Vielzahl der Datenjournalisten an eine unbestechliche, objektive Logik der computergestützten Datenauswertung, auf deren Basis autoritative und eindeutige Aussagen getroffen werden können. Auf der anderen Seite plädieren beide befragten Experten für einen Ausbau methodologischer Transparenz in datenjournalistischen Produkten, eine solche Präsentation der möglichen Schwachstellen der Betrachtungsweisen wäre bei einer Überzeugung von nicht anzuzweifelnden Ergebnissen der Analysen nicht notwendig. Aus konstruktivistischer Sicht kann den Experten eine Dogmenfeindlichkeit gegenüber der unter Datenjournalisten im Allgemeinen allerdings durchaus anzutreffenden Ansicht attestiert werden, mit der Fähigkeit der Datenanalyse die Wirklichkeit in unbestechlicher Weise abbilden zu können.

Beide Experten betonen, dass die Nutzung von großen Datensätzen den zweifellos in der Berichterstattung vorhandenen „blinden Fleck" perspektivischer Darstellung nicht abschaffen, aber zumindest verringern können: Dadurch, dass die Abbilder der Realität durch die Anreicherung von Berichterstattung mittels datenjournalistischer Methoden an Bandbreite zunehmen und empirische Belege journalistische Behauptungen zu bekräftigen vermögen, nähere sich die Berichterstattung schrittweise einer objektiven Wirklichkeit in Sachen Muster von Ereignissen und Korrektheit der Darstellung an.

Vor dem Hintergrund der Anreicherung, nicht der vollständigen Neuerfindung des Berufszweiges des Onlinejournalismus, kann somit trotz Visualisierungsmöglichkeiten und

---

[136] Vgl. Willis; S. 11; Z. 328 – 332.
[137] Waite; S. 14; Z. 417 – 420.

Interaktivitätsoptionen im Datenjournalismus nicht von einer grundsätzlich neuen Medienrealität gesprochen werden. Allerdings stellt die Option der „Annäherung an die Wirklichkeit" einen Hinweis auf die ideologische Überzeugung der Experten aus dem Lager des Realismus dar: Eine ontische Realität existiert und die Methoden, die in variierender Rigorosität bezüglich der wissenschaftlichen Korrektheit verwendet werden, können dabei helfen, sie tatsächlich abbilden zu können.

Von einer mächtigen Legitimation journalistischer Behauptungen durch die Verwendung statistischer Methoden und Belege gehen die befragten Experten allerdings nur bedingt aus. Letztlich können nur Korrektheit und Stichhaltigkeit in der Analyse einen wertvollen Beitrag zur Berichterstattung liefern, Daten zu Verwenden befinden Derek Willis und Matt demnach nicht als Selbstzweck. Wie bei einem menschlichen Interviewpartner, so die Experten, muss der Hintergrund der Daten als Quelle und Wachsamkeit beim Interviewen dieser an den Tag gelegt werden.

Ein grundsätzliches Vertrauen der befragten Datenjournalisten in empirisch-systematisch erhobene Daten und den sich daraus ergebenden Zusammenhängen lehnten diese zwar prinzipiell ab und kritisierten die im Berufsfeld der Datenjournalisten durchaus verbreitete Naivität gegenüber signifikanten Funden in großen Datenmengen. Auf der anderen Seite halten die Experten die datenjournalistischen Werkzeuge für eine durchaus vertrauenswürdige Erweiterung der notwendigen Fähigkeiten von Reportern.

Vor dem Hintergrund des Wettkampfs um Arbeitsplätze dürfte die kritische Haltung von Journalisten vielversprechenden Datensätzen gegenüber weiterhin hinten anstehen. In diesem Zusammenhang bezeugten die interviewten Experten die schon von Siegfried F. Schmidt prognostizierte Praxisblindheit eines Journalisten, der tagtäglich mit Datensätzen arbeitet und die Perspektivität und Beschränktheit dieser aus dem Blick verliert und das Vertrauen auf von anderen programmierte Werkzeuge, aufgrund einer Aversion gegen mathematische und programmiersprachliche Logik nicht in der Funktionsweise nachvollzogene Programme zum Erstellen von Geschichten als Gefahren für korrekte Berichterstattung.

Egoistische Motive der Reporter, an einem attraktiven und lukrativen Trend teilzuhaben ohne das notwendige „Know-How" aufzuweisen, könnten nach Ansicht der Experten Karrieren schnell beenden und bedeutsame, schwerwiegende Fehldeutungen von Zusammenhängen zur Folge haben. Auf lange Sicht dürften derartige Versuche, einen Trend ohne den notwendigen theoretischen Background zu nutzen, fehlschlagen, da nach Ansicht der Experten die methodologische Transparenz von datenjournalistischen Angeboten ein ausschlaggebendes Kriterium für deren Platzierung im marktwirtschaftlichen Wettbewerb darstellen wird.

6 Fazit

Die vorliegende Arbeit befasst sich mit der Fragestellung „Beeinflussen die Methoden des Datenjournalismus das Selbstbild von Journalisten in dem Sinne, dass sie objektivere Berichterstattung glauben?". Um die Forschungsfrage zu beantworten, wurden die amerikanischen Datenjournalisten, Programmierer und Dozenten Derek Willis und Matt Waite in einem Experteninterview nach ihren Ansichten zu dem Thema befragt. Die Aussagen der Experten wurden im Anschluss unter den Prämissen der im Vorfeld besprochenen theoretischen Perspektive des „diskursiven Konstruktivismus" untersucht.

Letztlich kann die Forschungsfrage nicht eindeutig beantwortet werden: Zwar sprachen viele Aussagen der Experten von einer Annäherung an objektive Wahrheiten. Auf der anderen Seite betonten beide Interviewpartner die Wichtigkeit methodologischer Transparenz und einer kritischen Haltung gegenüber den Daten an sich und den Analysemethoden.

In selbstkritischer Hinsicht müssen die vorliegende Arbeit und deren Autor anerkennen, dass die Durchführung und die Analyse der Ergebnisse der Experteninterviews, besonders aus konstruktivistischer Theorieperspektive, Mängel in der Umsetzung aufweisen, die auf fehlende Erfahrung in diesem Bereich zurückzuführen sind.

In weiterführender Forschung wäre die Überprüfung der gefundenen Ergebnisse mithilfe einer quantifizierenden Erhebung sinnvoll, die im Kontext dieser Arbeit forschungsökonomisch unmöglich war. Interessant wäre die Untersuchung der Haltungen verschiedener Mitglieder in einer (deutschen, vergleichend aber auch amerikanischen) Redaktion: Vom beratenden Web-Entwickler über den Reporter zum Chefredakteur werden sicher verschiedene Meinungen bezüglich methodologischer Transparenz und der Notwendigkeit dieser vertreten.

Auch eine Untersuchung aus normativer Sicht, die auf das Ausmaß wünschenswerter methodologischer Transparenz abzielt, wäre denkbar. Simon Rogers vom britischen Guardian plädiert angesichts der Zugänglichkeit der datenjournalistischen Methoden für eine „critical literacy", die zur Bekämpfung einiger Mythen, die um den Datenjournalismus herum entstanden sind, beitragen könnte. Seiner Meinung nach ersetzt ein interessanter Datensatz nicht die journalistische Beurteilung eines Themas nach seiner Relevanz, Datensätze können unvollständig, unpräzise, veraltet sowie in ihrer Aussagekraft bürokratisch-verengt sein und eine kritische, elaborierte Interpretation der eigenen Funde ist in jedem Fall notwendig.[138] Die Zugänglichkeit von Daten befähige nicht zwingendermaßen jedermann, kritischer Journalist werden zu können.[139] Eine „computer-literacy", also Programmiersprachen und statistische Arbeitsweisen zu beherrschen, gepaart mit dem inhaltlich-kritischen Blick eines Journalisten ist auch nach Lorenz Matzat für guten Datenjournalismus notwendig.[140]

Aus normativer Sicht könnte Transparenz, nicht aber Objektivität gefordert werden, wie Siegfried S. Schmidt betont: „Aber die Forderung nach objektiver Berichterstattung übersieht, daß Journalisten nicht mehr abverlangt werden kann als intellektuelle Redlichkeit und handwerklich bestmögliche Recherche."[141]

---

[138] Vgl. Rogers (2013): S. 273f.
[139] Vgl. Ebd.: S. 275.
[140] Vgl. Beckedahl (2011).
[141] Vgl. Schmidt (1994): S. 18.

Literatur

Bogner, Alexander und Wolfgang Menz (Hrsg.). 2009. Experteninterviews in der qualitativen Sozialforschung. Zur Einführung in eine sich intensivierende Methodendebatte. In *Experteninterviews. Theorien, Methoden, Anwendungsfelder*, Hrsg. Wolfgang Menz, 7 – 34. Wiesbaden: VS Verlag.

Beckedahl, Markus. 2011. *Gastbeitrag: Datenjournalismus und die Zukunft der Berichterstattung*. URL: https://netzpolitik.org/2011/gastbeitrag-datenjournalismus-und-die-zukunft-der-berichterstattung/. Zugegriffen: 08.09.2014.

Bradshaw, Paul. 2010. *How to be a data journalist. Data journalism trainer and writer Paul Bradshaw explains how to get started in data journalism, from getting to the data to visualising it.* URL: http://www.theguardian.com/news/datablog/2010/oct/01/data-journalism-how-to-guide. Zugegriffen: 08.09.2014.

Bunz, Mercedes. 2011. *Datenjournalismus: Wie digitalisiertes Wissen unser Verhältnis zur Wahrheit ändert.* URL: http://berlinergazette.de/mercedes-bunz-wikileaks-wahrheit-hannah-arendt/. Zugegriffen: 08.09.2014.

Dietrich, Daniel. 2010. *Data Driven Journalism: Versuch einer Definition.* URL: https://netzpolitik.org/2010/data-driven-journalism-versuch-einer-definition/. Zugegriffen: 08.09.2014.

Faulstich, Werner. 2004. *Medienwissenschaft*. Paderborn: Wilhelm Fink Verlag.

Fields, Robin. 2013. *From Shoe Leather to Big Data: ProPublica and the Future of Watchdog Journalism. Digital tools are reinvigorating watchdog reporting.* URL: http://www.nieman.harvard.edu/reports/article/102908/From-Shoe-Leather-to-Big-Data-ProPublica-and-the-Future-of-Watchdog-Journalism.aspx. Zugegriffen: 08.09.2014.

Gläser, Jochen und Grit Laudel. 2010. *Experteninterviews und qualitative Inhaltsanalyse als Instrumente rekonstruierender Untersuchungen.* Wiesbaden: VS Verlag.

Haller, Michael. 1994. Recherche und Nachrichtenproduktion als Konstruktionsprozesse. In *Die Wirklichkeit der Medien. Eine Einführung in die Kommunikationswissenschaft*, Hrsg. Klaus Merten, Siegfried J. Schmidt und Siegfried Weischenberg, 277 – 290. Opladen: Westdeutscher Verlag.

Holovaty, Adrian. 2006. *A fundamental way newspaper sites need to change*. URL: http://www.holovaty.com/writing/fundamental-change/. Zugegriffen: 08.09.2014.

Khatchadourian, Raffi. 2010. *No Secrets. Julian Assange's mission for total transparency.* URL: http://www.newyorker.com/magazine/2010/06/07/no-secrets. Zugegriffen: 08.09.2014.

Knight, Megan und Clare Cook. 2013. *Social Media for Journalists. Principles and Practice.* London: SAGE Publications Ltd.

Matzat, Lorenz. 2011. *Datenjournalismus.* URL: http://www.bpb.de/gesellschaft/medien/opendata/64069/datenjournalismus. Zugegriffen: 08.09.2014.

Meckel, Miriam, Christian Fieseler und Stephanie Grubenmann. 2012. *Social Media – Chancen und Herausforderungen für den Journalismus.* URL: https://www.alexandria.unisg.ch/export/DL/219051.pdf. Zugegriffen: 08.09.2014.

Pürer, Heinz. 2003. *Publizistik- und Kommunikationswissenschaft. Ein Handbuch.* Konstanz: UVK.

Pörksen, Bernhard. 2011. Schlüsselwerke des Konstruktivismus. Eine Einführung. In *Schlüsselwerke des Konstruktivismus*, Hrsg. Bernhard Pörksen, 13 – 30. Wiesbaden: VS Verlag.

Pörksen, Bernhard. 2006. *Die Beobachtung des Beobachters. Eine Erkenntnistheorie der Journalistik.* Konstanz: UVK.

Rogers, Simon. 2013. *Facts are sacred. The power of data.* London: Faber and Faber Limited.

Rusbridger, Alan. 2010. *The splintering of the fourth estate. Media organizations are trying various routes to the future – the Guardian's is firmly an open and collaborative one.* URL: http://www.theguardian.com/commentisfree/2010/nov/19/open-collaborative-future-journalism. Zugegriffen: 08.09.2014.

Pew Research Center. 2014. *The Growth in Digital Reporting. What it means for Journalism and News Consumers.* URL: http://www.journalism.org/files/2014/03/Shifts-in-Reporting_For-uploading.pdf. Zugegriffen: 08.09.2014.

Pew Research Center. 2014. *State of the News Media. Overview.* URL: http://www.journalism.org/files/2014/03/Overview.pdf. Zugegriffen: 08.09.2014.

Scholl, Armin. 2011. Die Wirklichkeit der Medien. Armin Scholl über den Konstruktivismus in der Kommunikations- und Medienwissenschaft. In *Schlüsselwerke des Konstruktivismus*, Hrsg. Bernhard Pörksen, 443 – 462. Wiesbaden: VS Verlag.

Schmidt, Siegfried J. 1994. Die Wirklichkeit des Beobachters. In *Die Wirklichkeit der Medien. Eine Einführung in die Kommunikationswissenschaft*, Hrsg. Klaus Merten, Siegfried J. Schmidt und Siegfried Weischenberg, 3 – 19. Opladen: Westdeutscher Verlag.

Thibodeaux, Troy. 2011. *5 tips for getting started in data journalism.* URL: http://www.poynter.org/how-tos/digital-strategies/147734/5-tips-for-getting-started-in-data-journalism/. Zugegriffen: 08.09.2014.

Thibodeaux, Troy. 2011. *10 tools that can help data journalists do better work, be more efficient.* URL: http://www.poynter.org/how-tos/digital-strategies/147736/10-tools-for-the-data-journalists-tool-belt/. Zugegriffen: 08.09.2014.

Anhang

Leitfaden für die Experteninterviews (Stand: 07.08.2014)

a. Hello! Nice to meet you, Mr. xxx. Thanks for taking your time to talk to me! I'll have to record this conversation to be able to work with it later. Is that okay for you?

b. Shall we just start right away or do you have any questions?

c. Your Site on the homepage of the xxx says you're an interactive developer slash journalist with xxx. Could you explain to me, what exactly is your job there?

d. So just to get the gist, what steps or stages make up the process of a typical "hybrid journalism" story? Is there an archetype for a "Upshot"-story?

e. Simon Rogers from the guardian says in his book that reporting based on data is the new "industry trend" everyone has to adapt to, do you agree?

f. What are the attractive elements in data journalism?

g. Taking a respectable source of the data as a given, do you feel there's a new kind of "truth" in massive data, that journalists should report about?

h. Do data, given a source you can trust, add legitimacy to journalistic claims?

i. Is there a sort of "new objectivity" that data journalists are fond of using?

j. Can data journalism reduce the "blind spots" so to speak in journalism? Broaden the range of picturing the reality?

k. To what extend do data journalists have to be programming "geeks" so to speak?

l. Are there any data journalists who are less geeky in terms of programming and just use the tools someone else develops?

m. Do data journalists trust the tools others program for them?

n. How to data journalists reflect the "cybernetic" origin of their findings with their tools? Do they just trust a statistic significance?

o. The methods of data journalism are derived from scientific contexts, why don't data journalists make the same effort when it comes to the transparency of the process of storytelling like a scientist writing a paper?

Telefon- Interview mit Matt Waite, Datenjournalist und Professor of Practice at the College of Journalism and Mass Communications an der University of Nebraska-Lincoln am 07. August 2014. Teilnehmer: Wilke Bitter als Interviewer (Im Folgenden mit „F" wie Fragender benannt) und Matt Waite (Im Folgenden mit „A" wie Antwortender benannt). Aus Platzgründen sind Eingangs- und Abschiedsgespräch nicht im Transcript enthalten.

1   // 00:01:26

2   F: Your Site on the homepage of the College of Journalism and Mass Communication says in
3   2007 you've begun working as a hybrid journalist/programmer, making the most of both your
4   programming and reporting skills. Could you explain to me as sort of a layman, what steps or
5   stages make up the process of a typical "hybrid journalism" story?

6   // 00:01:55

7   A: Sure.

8   F: Where do you start, what's the finishing line?

9   // 00:02:07

10   A: It always starts with a story. When you're a reporter, you're out talking to people, you're
11   hearing about stuff, you're reading things, you're digging in government documents and stuff
12   like that. The best stories always start with some thing – some story nugget. Some "Huh –
13   isn't that interesting." Some element that peaks your curiosity. And then the process is using
14   whatever tools you need to use to get that story done. And being able to program, being able
15   to write some code is really just an extension of that, in my view. Now there's two kinds of
16   programmer journalists. There's people who started out as programmers who have maybe
17   worked in the software industry, who became interested in journalism and come to it later. I
18   think they kind of approach it as "programmers first, journalists second". I started out as a
19   journalist and learned how to program along the way, so I kind of approached it as "journalist
20   first, programmer second". And frankly, the differences are extremely subtle if not completely
21   invisible most of the time. I see stories by friends of mine who are programmers first that I
22   say "Oh I probably wouldn't have handled it that way, I probably would have gone in another
23   direction and that's fine. I can do that with just straight reporters, too. So don't get me wrong,
24   there's not a huge distinction there. Where the programming comes into play is, you might

25   need to download every document in a document repository on a government website. And it
26   might be paginated, you might have 50 entries on one page, click on the next button it goes to
27   50 entries on the next page, so on and so forth. Well, sitting there and clicking on that and
28   downloading each one manually, clicking next and doing it again, that's insane, you don't
29   want to do that. You can write some code that can do that. There are some tools that are out
30   there that you can download every document on a page with, browser extensions, things like
31   that. Being able to take the mundane tasks of reporting, of gathering information, of
32   automatically going and grabbing something and automating that and letting a computer do
33   what a computer is good at is what I think where the real muscle is. In being able to marry
34   your journalism and your programming skills together and do good things.

35   F: It's maybe like not being in the stone age anymore and taking your journalism into the
36   present.

37   // 00:05:19

38   A: I talk about robotics. Using automation and robotics are kind of an extension of the
39   reporter. Almost like a reporting exoskeleton. I'm a big sci-fi-nerd. But, you know, trying to
40   build bionic extensions of the journalists to do these things. And I think that's ultimately
41   where we're going to go. Build systems that will monitor crime reports 24 hours a day, 7 days
42   a week. They just alert us when something interesting is going on because we'll have program
43   and algorithm that determine when something's interesting. Or with campaign contributions,
44   money given to politics which is a bigger deal here in the U.S. than in other places. But you
45   can do the same thing to public opinion polling. You can record public opinion polling during
46   an election and have the algorithm flag a term when the public opinion polling change to a
47   certain threshold. You can be focusing on a different thing than watching polls all the time.

48   F: Okay. The next question would be: Are you still active in that kind of work, are you still
49   active as a journalist/programmer, do you still report for any kind of publication?

50   // 00:06:51

51   A: Not in traditional media. I don't do stories anymore. Not because I don't want to, I really
52   do, I miss it. It's because I don't have time right now. I'm so very active in this intersection of
53   journalism and programming. The classes I teach, at least half of them involve that. I do teach
54   a "beginning of reporting" class every so often. I incorporate elements of data journalism into
55   it. I teach, you know, beginning spreadsheets and I show student journalists how to find data

56   on certain things and do some really basic math with excel to find a trend or see something
57   interesting in a data set. And I bring that to our very "beginning of reporting" classes. For
58   instance this fall I'm teaching a class about how to write software that can generate a story.
59   How you can do algorithmic story generation.

60   F: Okay, we'll get to that later. I've got these questions in a very specific order. I find that
61   very interesting but we'll have to put that on a hold for just another second. You just
62   mentioned the trend that "should" go in the direction of computer assisted reporting. Do you
63   feel like it's necessary or it's inevitable, the trend towards…

64   // 00:08:47

65   A: It's absolutely inevitable. The reasons are very very simple. The amount of data that is
66   available in our world in the last five years has increased at an almost unimaginable rate. You
67   can't really be a journalist without dealing with that data in some way. And if you can't deal
68   with it on your own, you will now be holding onto people who can and that doesn't make you
69   a very good journalist.

70   F: So you don't really have the choice if you want to be on top of your game, so to speak.

71   // 00:09:35

72   A: Not at all.

73   F: Okay, so that sounds a little bit negative. But what are the attractive elements in data
74   journalism? What are the perks of it?

75   // 00:09:52

76   A: Well, I will grant you that I probably come off as a little harsh on that. But understand that
77   I have been talking about data journalism since maybe the late 90s. And I've been telling
78   people: "Look! The data is there, it's coming! You'll be able to do all these amazing things
79   with it. You really need to learn how to do this stuff. And I've been saying that since 1998
80   and I still get a lot of the same reactions that I got then. I don't know. I've kind of gone past
81   the point of being about the carrot, I'm more about the stick now: "Look, If you're not using
82   it, you're left behind. There's nothing I can do for you anymore, I'm sorry.". But the
83   advantages are many. The simplest and most direct is that you'll be able to do stories that
84   other people can't do. You'll be able to do stories that are impossible to do with a pencil and a
85   notebook and your own two feet and going to talking to people. You'll be able to see the

86   world in more complete and empirical ways. Your stories will have a foundation that's much
87   stronger than they would with, you know, four anecdotes and a bunch of interviews. And not
88   only that, the kind of things your story can do will increase massively because you'll have the
89   ability to do data visualizations, you'll have the ability to do interactive, you'll have the
90   ability to add data tools to your story that let people explore the data on their own. The world
91   is made up of individuals, individual people who have their own interests and their own biases
92   and own concerns and being able to give them a tool that lets them explore specifically what's
93   interesting to them while being able to read a story that you've done that shows why this is
94   broadly applicable to them is a really powerful way to get someone interested in a subject.
95   And you can't do that, you can't do that with traditional journalism. It's just impossible. So
96   it's the world of possibilities that opens up to you when you involve data in journalism that it
97   think is the real selling point of it.

98   F: Okay. Now those are the perks and of course there's the other side of the medal, too. The
99   sources for example, where you get the data from. Taking a respectable source as a given, do
100   you think that there's not just a whole new range of information you can process but the
101   information you can process has some kind of new "truth" in it? In this massive data, that data
102   journalism should report about? Is there also a semantic difference to traditional journalism,
103   do you think?

104   // 00:13:43

105   A: Yeah, actually, you're hitting on something I've really gotten interested in lately.

106   F: Yeah, me too.

107   // 00:13:53

108   A: And that is this kind of belief that I see on the part of a lot of data journalists that because
109   there is data, it does mean that it is true. That a data set is, you know, that a data set just is. It
110   doesn't have a point of view. It doesn't have a bias. It doesn't have flaws. Because there are
111   numbers, that means that it is correct. And that's just not the case. It's absolutely not the case.
112   And I think that journalists should be, I stress should be, in a proper position here because
113   we're accustomed to interviewing human sources whom we know have biases and a point of
114   view and are selfish and, you know, are wanting to make themselves look good or make
115   someone else look bad. People have their own kind of agenda here. And to believe that data
116   doesn't is a huge mistake. Data is gathered for a reason. And it's gathered generally by people

117 for a reason. And those decisions, those subjective decisions that go into it will shape and
118 mould the data and it may provide an answer that's accurate in the sense that that's what the
119 data says, but it's not the truth. It's not what actually occurs. And without you being able to
120 parse that out and to think about it to understand what it is that you're working with, you're
121 going to make huge mistakes. You're going to say things about the world that just aren't true.
122 I describe it as "blind faith". It's people walking around with almost a kind of religious fervor
123 that they're saying "Well..". I could take a million bible verses, take the word god and put
124 data in and it would actually work.

125 F: That sounds interesting.

126 // 00:16:14

127 A: It kind of disturbs me a little bit. You know, people walking around thinking that data is
128 all-knowing, all-seeing. The truth is, it's completely the opposite. So yeah, what it does do is
129 it argues for a new sense of skepticism on the part of the journalists. But it's rooted in a very
130 old set of skepticism that we have. It's not a reflex that's totally new to us.

131 F: Do you think that this sort of skepticism is already there inside the minds of most data
132 journalists you know or is that a trend that has not reached the bulk of data journalists yet? Do
133 they still think that there still is this ultimate, objective truth inside the data that they can just
134 pluck and plug into their stories?

135 // 00:17:20

136 A: I think what you're seeing now is a flood of new people into this space. Data journalism
137 has become very hot and popular and interesting and it's drawing in new people. And you're
138 seeing people who haven't had a lot of time to get burned, really. To have worked on a story,
139 only to find out later that the data is complete garbage. And the other thing you're seeing is,
140 you're seeing some very high profile efforts out there – VOX specifically, but also Five-
141 Thirtyeight. I'm gonna lump them in there although they don't do nearly as much as VOX
142 does, but the New York Times' Upshot blog. They are all this very high-profile entrance into
143 this new place. And Five-Thirtyeight and VOX are making some really bad mistakes. They're
144 doing it from a place of faith in data. Because there is data, that must mean it's true. VOX is
145 even going a step further and doing some kind of "eyewitness-ride on tour"-things. I don't
146 know what I said here, but this makes no sense. Can you cut a small piece of audio for me so I
147 can hear it? Borrowing other people's maps and taking other people's graphics and putting

148   them in there. They've only recently begun linking back to the original source material which
149   is really kind of odious but the whole thing is that I just think that they haven't had something
150   yanked out from under them yet. They haven't been burned by a data set yet. There's an old
151   set of journalists working in data journalism since the 80s who know what I'm talking about
152   with doubt and disbelief and caution and making sure that the data says what it says and it
153   comports with reality and things like that. There's a whole new set of folks. And that haven't
154   gotten through there yet. They haven't developed that sense yet. So, is it there? Yeah, I do
155   believe it's there. I think it's that we journalists know that they should be doubtful about but I
156   think there's this rush right now to make a name and to get stuff on the thing. Post on the new
157   data journalism site and do it fast and do it more than the other people. That kind of sense of
158   doubt is not really being allowed to set in. Someone's got to screw up something really bad
159   and that would be catastrophic for them. That's when everybody's going to go: "Okay, maybe
160   we are to slow down here just a little bit and think about what we're doing."

161   F: Okay, that's quite exactly the point my bachelor thesis is headed to. Let's just continue
162   with my questionnaire. But on the other side, if you let this bias out of the game, there is a sort
163   of possibility or power inside data to give journalistic claims a little bit of legitimacy, if you
164   use it right, would you say?

165   // 00:21:18

166   A: Yeah, absolutely. Having been in journalism and now being in academia where people
167   take rigor in a kind of methodology in a much much more seriously than we do in a
168   newsroom. Yeah, I think there's a real opportunity there to really improve the stature of
169   reporting. I think that the media have a well earned but not entirely fair reputation right now, a
170   low reputation. And I think that data journalism could do a lot to improve that and now I'm
171   not going to say that it's going to solve everything because there are still going to be stupid
172   people doing stupid things. And trying to make a name for themselves by cutting corners and
173   getting caught and bringing disrepute to the whole business but the possibilities for more rigor
174   are a huge thing and I think it's something we ought to take more seriously. Now because of
175   the deadlines of newsrooms, because of the need to publish and the need to get stuff out there,
176   it's going to be a limited opportunity but I think we should begin to develop workflows and
177   the norm is programmatic. I don't mean in the sense of writing code. I mean it in the sense of
178   creating program, creating a system of operation around making sure things are correct and
179   using this kind of scientific method. Form a hypothesis and test it with data and look at the
180   results and see that it is repeatable within the results. Using the scientific method as a means

181   to journalism is an old idea as well that goes back to the 70s actually with Phil Meyer and the
182   new "precision journalism". He's been talking about the scientific method since not to long
183   after I was born. But the more we get into data and into data journalism the opportunities are
184   there I think that we should be talking about the scientific method and we should be talking
185   about rigor and we should be talking about doing things that would at least take a step toward
186   withstanding peer review on that kind of academic stage. I'm not saying that we should do
187   that because it's impossible on newsroom deadlines. But we should at least acknowledge it
188   and take a step toward it. Because I think it would do a lot to improve our reputation as an
189   industry. I did a story on wetlands loss in Florida that used remote sensing and ultimately we
190   published our complete methodology online. And the methodology was actually longer than
191   the story itself and it could have withstood peer review. It did go out for a limited peer review,
192   I send the methodology out to several professors around country who did remote syncing
193   work and they looked at it and said: "Yeah, this would work. If you did these things and you
194   followed this then this would work." I don't think you could do this on every story but I think
195   we should do on some.

196   F: So these scientific methods you're using to generate or to present stories or to make them
197   up, is there some sort of new objectivity that data journalism can bring into the business?
198   Because those scientific methods are always prone to be leaving the spectator out of the thing
199   and claiming to be objective. Do you think that that is correct?

200   // 00:25:47

201   A: I think you just hit on the fray, the awful phrase here and that's claiming to be objective. I
202   don't believe there is true objectivity. I don't think it's possible. I think we are human beings
203   and we are all flawed in our own way and we all bring something to the table. Pure
204   objectivity, even in the sciences, is impossible. There are legions of cases where researchers,
205   attempting to do the right thing and being scientifically pure have put their finger on the scale
206   and through their scientific methods have come up with results that weren't true science
207   because they didn't want to look bad or some human impulse led them to do that. I think we
208   can take a step toward of what I think a scientific method in data journalism is wants to do
209   which is trying to do reach a new kind of authority. Not necessarily objectivity but authority,
210   allowing us to make a claim and write a declarative statement based on something other than
211   the word of other people.

212　F: Do you think that this opinion of yours is shared by data journalists? Or do most of them
213　think "This is the thing, we're using scientific methods and this is the truth right here, buy
214　it!'"?

215　// 00:27:29

216　A: Uh, in varying degrees. I think if you asked a hundred journalists, whether or not
217　objectivity exists, you get a hundred different answers somewhere along the line here. You
218　know, on the left would be there is such a thing as pure objectivity and I am doing it. On the
219　right would be there is no such thing as objectivity and we should abandon it completely. And
220　I think you'll find people kind of swirling around the middle of those two poles and they slide
221　along that line really day by day. I've met one person who is adamantly and devoutly of the
222　mind that objectivity is dead, it never existed in the first place. We should get rid of it, we
223　should stop talking about it. It's a waste of time, to hell with it. I've really only met one
224　person of that end of the stick. Most people are somewhere in the realm of "objectivity is a
225　good thing and we should strive for it, even though we're going to come up short". And I
226　think data journalism is in that kind of same realm of "yes, data allows us to be more
227　authoritative, it allows us to say things more authoritatively with less regard to the bias of the
228　individual but we still bring a point of view to it and the way we write it could change things
229　so pure objectivity is impossible but it's still a pretty good thing".

230　F: That's very interesting actually. I've forgotten one question about the perks of data
231　journalism. I read a lot about "blind spots" in theory of reporting, that you can only have your
232　focus on one thing. And data journalism always claims to have no such thing as a focus
233　because you can tweak the in every which way you want. Is that a view that is shared by data
234　journalists, that you don't have any blank spots anymore because you can broaden the range
235　of reality you want to picture so much?

236　// 00:30:21

237　A: If it is held by data journalists I would like to disabuse them of that notion. I don't think
238　that you have data means that you don't have blind spots. Blind spots are an inherently human
239　thing. You can be so laser-focused on trying to prove any given point that you might miss all
240　of the other things in there. I don't think that data helps you with blind spots and I don't know
241　if it necessarily hurts you with them either. The blind spots that are there are the ones you
242　bring to the table. I often talk to students about how data is a source. And using data
243　journalism is just interviewing a source. You are interviewing data. You are asking questions

that are kind of in a weird, stilted language but you're still asking it questions. If you're not asking the right questions or if you're asking the wrong questions, you will get the wrong answer or you'll get a limited answer or you won't get the whole answer. And so you've got to really empty your head when you're approaching it and just look at what's there. I do a whole talk about this area of Buddhist teaching to have a beginner's mind. And that you should have the approach to things like this with the mind of a child. That this is the first time you're seeing. That being an expert in something is actually really bad. As an expert you have an opinion about things, you have an opinion about what's important and what's not. And you will, in the process of doing that, maybe consciously or subconsciously, ignore things because you believe that they aren't important. And by doing that you open up blind spots. I don't think data journalism necessarily helps or hurts with blind spots, I think the blind spots are what you bring into it.

F: Okay. Asking the data questions, interviewing the data, is that a new challenge to upcoming journalists? Do journalists who want to make it in the field have to be "programming geeks" so to speak?

// 00:32:56

A: No, I don't think so. I think 80 percent of the data journalism that I do... I just talked to a bunch of journalism professors about that – they're all scared to death that they'll have to learn python and R and SAS and all this crazy stuff and I went "Look, 80 percent of the data journalism that I do is in Microsoft Excel. It's just a spreadsheet, it's just a couple of sorts, it's a Min-Max, it's a median or an average or something like that. We're not doing multivariate regressions here, we're not doing differential calculus. It's pretty basic stuff. And the tools to do that are pretty simple to learn." Where journalism students fall down and where I think journalists in general fall down is that, at least here in the U.S. and I have seen this elsewhere, including Germany, journalists seem to be math-phobic. They tend to be afraid of math and numbers. The German kind of pre-college education system does a much better job at teaching you than here in the U.S. my experience with particularly European journalists is that they have a much better grasp on math and numeracy than Americans do, owing to their education system. But the fact still remains that journalists by large are "word-people", they're storytellers they are people who are comfortable writing. And math is a different skill set and they are less comfortable with it if not outright afraid of it. That's a problem. That's a real problem if you're doing data journalism because the questions you're asking are based in logic, they're based in numbers and they are based in math. And that math might be primary

277 school math – calculating an average, when did you start doing that? When you were twelve
278 years old or even younger than that. If you have followed sports at all in life you've probably
279 have come across an average in there somewhere I mean you have the tools to understand
280 what it is. Where data journalism comes along is where you might want to apply an average
281 or an median to a data set where somebody hasn't done that before and you have to
282 understand the fundamental difference between an average and a median and what those
283 answers will tell you and how they are influenced by extremes on either end of the number
284 scale and things like that. That's where a lot of journalists fall down. It's that kind of logical
285 and mathematical thinking. I'm an advocate here for increasing the amount of math and
286 numeracy and statistics education within our journalism program but I can tell you that the
287 students that I have in class are adamantly opposed to that, they are deathly afraid of having to
288 go take a college level statistics course because that's not what they've signed up for. And I
289 try to tell them yeah, well, the world says you're wrong and the modern age that we live in
290 says "buckle up kid, you'll have to learn some statistics!"

291 F: But it's not just simple spreadsheets or a median or an average that are used in data
292 journalism. There's also this whole range of very much more complex tools, isn't there. And
293 are those math-afraid journalists who still want to use those data journalism tools, are they
294 sometimes in the situation that they have to use tools that they don't quite understand and just
295 have to trust the mechanics inside them?

296 // 00:37:15

297 A: Yeah, that does happen and it is an extremely dangerous thing. I have described that as
298 being children with loaded guns. You know, you hand a bunch of loaded guns to a
299 kindergarten class and bad things are going to happen. So, that does happen. And where that
300 kind of predicted meltdown is going to occur, as I said before, somebody is going to do
301 something completely career-limiting. Honestly, I think it's going to be in that kind of
302 neighborhood. It's going to be "I figured out the right combination of buttons to push in R to
303 do some kind of complex regression analysis and I didn't have any idea of what I was doing
304 but it told me the answer that I thought I should get. And here it is!" And it's going to be
305 completely wrong and somebody's going to look at it and go "What?!" And that's going to be
306 it.

307 F: But that's not the case in a broad level yet?

308 // 00:38:26

309 A: No, it's not. The kind of applications for those really complex tools are still fairly limited.
310 Most of the things the kind of day-to-day journalists are going to be using are actually quite
311 simple. I mean the most complicated things we'll get into will be maybe some linear algebra,
312 maybe, well, the Sun Sentinel in Florida won the Pulitzer Price using like junior high level
313 physics. Looking at distance equals rate times time. And they figured out how to catch police
314 officers speeding between toll booths on a toll road because they had the distance between the
315 two toll booths and they had the time that it took them to get from one to the other and then
316 they could calculate the rate they had. And they caught them exceedingly fast, like Autobahn
317 level speeding which is not legal here in the United States. They were off duty and all kinds of
318 things like that. They were doing, I can't do the Kilometer per hours calculations in my head
319 but they were doing over 100 miles an hour here. So way way, 45 miles per hour over the
320 speed limit – you know, exceedingly fast. But that is high school, early education level
321 physics and algebra. They had two of the three variables in the equation and were able to
322 figure out the other one.

323 F: And the sources of those data were public in the U.S.? Public data that is just published by
324 some administration?

325 // 00:40:27

326 A: Well, they weren't published, they had to go get them. They used open records laws in
327 Florida which are extremely good in Florida to pry that information loose. Those police cars
328 had prepaid toll transponders on them that paid the toll for the toll road automatically through
329 a sensor and that recorded the data. The state had the data. So they could go and request the
330 toll data for each of the transponders in police cars and then they had everything they needed
331 at that point.

332 F: So there's some data you could not question, some that is just mechanically recorded, and
333 that's the data you can really trust?

334 // 00:41:14

335 A: Well, no actually, I mean, to an extent you can. You can say that the data itself, you can
336 say that between this point and this point on this date this police officer was driving a hundred
337 miles an hour. That is completely true. What it is utterly lacking from that moment is the
338 context in that moment. Was that person on duty in that moment? Were they in pursuit of a
339 criminal suspect that was fleeing and driving a 105 miles per hour? You don't know if there is

340   a legitimate reason for them to be doing that. There is a very very small number of legitimate

341   reasons to be doing that but just because the data says this person was doing a hundred miles

342   per hour between point a and point b does not necessarily mean that there wasn't a reason for

343   them to be doing that.

344   F: Is that a thing that comes up in the articles about it? Is this reflection of their own methods

345   a part of data journalism stories?

346   // 00:42:33

347   A: I think it has to be.

348   F: Yeah, it has to be but is it?

349   // 00:42:37

350   A: When you are accusing a law enforcement officer of criminal behavior, you need to be as

351   transparent as possible with your methods and data and your doubts and your caveats and all

352   of that. I mean what the Sun Sentinel went and did was they requested all of the timesheets of

353   those officers to figure out when and when not they were on duty and they eliminated all of

354   them who were on duty to have some legitimate claim to be speeding for law enforcement and

355   they still were able to find thousands and thousands of examples of police officers driving

356   exceedingly fast off duty when they were not, a lot of them, not even their own jurisdiction. I

357   mean, it would be a police officer driving extremely fast in Munich when they were from

358   Berlin. You know, not a reason to be doing it at all. Caught dead, red handed, not at all an

359   excuse here. So that's what they were looking for, an unassailable one. And to do that, they

360   had to do a lot of reporting to eliminate the data that was true, but in the context not accurate.

361   So even with that automated data you still have to ask "Ok, why and what were the

362   circumstances when that occurred?" Where that kind of eliminated is maybe weather data,

363   when you've got a sensor that is maybe detecting temperature or something like that where

364   context is really not going to matter…

365   F: Are you still there?

366   // 00:44:30

367   A: Yeah, sorry, there was a notification on my iPad and I got distracted.

368   F: No problem, you just said that there should be the reflection of methods in data journalism,

369   what are maybe the motives or what sort of stops them from doing all this transparency stuff

370 we have to do in a scientific context? Is there something that is maybe too much work for
371 them to be transparent?

372 // 00:45:18

373 A: The old excuse used to be that it's going into print and newsprint was expensive and there
374 wasn't enough space for it and so we can't do that. Well, the internet kind of blew that out of
375 the water, completely eliminated that as a concern.

376 F: Of course.

377 // 00:45:39

378 A: Ultimately, I think it is time. I think there are news agencies that rather spend time on the
379 story and not creating some kind of methodological explanation. I think that has to stop, we
380 have to be more serious about that. I think there should be a general, linear increase in the
381 amount of attention you pay to methodology in relation to the seriousness of the claims that
382 you are making. If you're doing a story, you know "The 10 funnest cities in your country, and
383 there's a crapload of those kind of "listicles" and stories out there right now, that, you know,
384 do you need to be methodologically pure and ultra-transparent about it – err, I mean, I would
385 but you know, let's not get over board with that.

386 F: But that's not the thing, that would be your own opinion about "funny". This connection
387 between the claim for objectivity and a scientific accuracy in reporting, that doesn't really
388 keep up in data journalism stories with the methodology, in my opinion. Is it maybe not just
389 time that keeps them from analyzing their own methods and maybe spotting the "blind spots"
390 that they have or is it, what we've talked about, the trust in the "truthworthiness" of the results
391 that come out of scientific methods?

392 // 00:47:32

393 A: I think if we were able to figure out some kind of way to measure this, you know, we could
394 do a mass survey of journalists and do some kind of regression here, I think most of the
395 variants that can be explained would be time first, second, I would call it laziness – "I've got
396 another story on, I'm not going to take time for this.", third I think there is a certain level of
397 not wanting to look, of not wanting to question things, just being done and move on – "It's
398 not that important or interesting to me." I think there's a heavy dose of human judgment that
399 goes in there that's not particularly healthy but I would also argue that lurking down in there

400 in those kind of variables are... There are a number of data journalists out there who have
401 only just recently learned how to analyze some data, they might not have or probably didn't
402 learn how to look critically at what they did an being able to take a step back and ask
403 informed and sharp questions about the methods they used in order to do what they did and
404 are ill-equipped to provide a truly transparent methodology to what they did. It is also
405 something that journalists are wholly unaccustomed to doing – traditional journalism doesn't
406 require you to do this. It doesn't require you to list your sources, it doesn't require you to
407 discuss your methods. And few if any journalism schools, training grounds for journalists, are
408 doing that or even talking about it, so there are a whole lot of variables that go into that but
409 primarily it's time.

410 F: Okay, I guess that's about it. I guess a closing word would be that those who are to
411 sanction bad reports without reflection of the methodology is probably the public, maybe the
412 readers should sort of request the transparency and just not read the stories that aren't
413 scientifically transparent?

414 // 00:50:30

415 A: Yeah, I think that's ultimately where it's going to be. I don't think there's any journalism
416 organization that's going to come along and start hammering people for doing that, I think it's
417 going to be the marketplace that's going to do that. The marketplace will, I believe, I hope, I
418 sincerely pray, the marketplace will see non-serious, non-rigorous journalism, they will be
419 duped by stories and they will ultimately feel put off by that and they will respond to it by no
420 longer going to that news organization and then that news organization will cease to exist. It
421 will be very Darwinian, the strongest and the most adaptable will survive and the weak and
422 the unwilling to change will die off and we'll be left with a stronger set of journalists. That's
423 my hope and I don't know if it will actually occur but it will be interesting to see how a lot of
424 those data journalism efforts shake out, who's going to survive. Is it the serious or is it the
425 ones that are just stealing other people's stuff, that are just throwing stuff out there and not
426 really are doing things that are kind of methodologically pure and end up caught doing it.

427 F: Two very interesting scenarios, that we are about to see. That's about it.

428 // 00:52:09

Telefon- Interview mit Derek Willis, Datenjournalist und Programmierer bei der New York Times am 14. August 2014. Teilnehmer: Wilke Bitter als Interviewer (Im Folgenden mit „F" wie Fragender benannt) und Derek Willis (Im Folgenden mit „A" wie Antwortender benannt). Aus Platzgründen sind Eingangs- und Abschiedsgespräch nicht im Transcript enthalten.

1   // 00:00:44

2   F: Your Site on the homepage of the Georgetown University says you're an interactive
3   developer "slash" with the New York Times. Could you explain to me what exactly is your
4   job there, your niche, so to say, in the NYT collective.

5   // 00:01:03

6   A: Sure. I started at the times about six and a half year ago as part of a group of developers in
7   the newsroom. I have a reporting background myself but I'm more on the geekier end of
8   reporting I guess you might say. I always like to work on data and with numbers so I got into
9   web development while I was at the Washington Post, which is where I was before the New
10 York Times. So when I came to the times I was part of a newsroom developers that worked
11 on things like election results and large projects that involve lots of data. Currently, since just
12 the beginning of the year, I moved to a new unit at the Times called the Upshot, which is a
13 sort of a more empirical approach to reporting. So what I do there, I guess one of the ways I
14 would describe it is that I interview data as well as people. I look for stories in data and in my
15 particular case political data and election data and then I write stories based on or sort of
16 guided by that data and the analysis. I still, obviously, talk to people and interview people but
17 I spend a lot more time, I think, sort of looking for stories and trying to build systems,
18 software systems, that help me find stories in data.

19 F: Yeah, that's just about what I read about you, too. So the Upshot is a brand new thing in
20 data journalism or is it just the outcome from an ongoing process that is just actual?

21 // 00:02:53

22 A: I think it's more of the latter, more of the sort of natural outcome of where journalism has
23 been going. I mean, working with data, doing stories that based off on data isn't terribly new
24 in journalism. And there's a relatively small group of people who do it in the United States
25 but I think it's something that has become that is seen as something more valuable,

26 increasingly more valuable. And also it's, you know, we're also getting just more and more
27 data, you know, in our lives all the time. Governments are producing more data, businesses
28 are producing more data, if you have a smartphone, you're producing more data yourself. So
29 there's a need for journalism in general and journalists in general to have some sort of
30 familiarity and skill in terms of working with data. And I think, you know, in some respects I
31 wish maybe we could have the Upshot be, you know, it wouldn't necessarily be just a small,
32 self-contained thing at the times but what we're trying to do is, we're trying to work with
33 other desks and work with other folks to sort of spread that knowledge and spread all those
34 techniques throughout the newsroom, because I can't think of any desks or any type of beings
35 that wouldn't benefit from that kind of approach.

36 F: The next question that I have written down is, just to get the gist, what steps or stages make
37 up the process of a typical hybrid journalism story, is there maybe an archetype for you
38 Upshot guys to produce a story like that? You told me about those applications that generate
39 stories or help you generate them, from the start to the finishing line, what's in there?

40 // 00:05:17

41 A: So, most of what we try to do is probably a little bit more of explaining or helping people
42 navigate the news rather than breaking the news I would say. There is some original,
43 breaking, original news, investigative type of stuff that we do. But I would say what we try to
44 do is, we try to look for things, themes in the news, ideas, concepts in the news that we can
45 actually explain or elaborate on in an empirical way. So for example, we're in the middle of a
46 legislative election's campaign season here in the United States. We've had a couple of
47 interesting and close elections, particularly in the state of Mississippi and so there's been a lot
48 of things written and reported about those elections but one of the things we tried to do after
49 there was a primary election and then a run-off, following the primary, one of the things we
50 tried to do as quickly as we could was to get the precinct level, the little election district
51 results. Get those data, gather them, compare them to previous elections and be able to say:
52 "Look, here is exactly how this particulate candidate, in this case Thad Cochran, here is how
53 he won this election." And because anecdotally, most people either guessed at it or did some
54 reporting that would sort of suggest that's the case, but what we were able to do is to sort of
55 come in and say: "Now, here's really what happened and we know that because we've looked
56 at the data, we've compared it to other, you know, previous elections in the same state, in the
57 same counties." And we were able to actually put a more definitive pronunciation on that.

58 And I think for me at least that is a really good use of our time, our efforts to go from the
59 anecdotal to the definitive, even when definitive refutes the anecdotal.

60 F: That means you've started with the data and looked into the data and compared it to what
61 happened to you in your daily journalism life and then you sort of have this new explaining
62 perspective that you can use.

63 // 00:07:44

64 A: Right.

65 F: Ok, next question, Simon Rogers, you may know him from the Guardian, says in his book
66 "Facts are sacred" that reporting based on data is the new industry standard and this trend is
67 something everyone in the business has to adapt to. Do you agree?

68 // 00:08:10

69 A: I would say I would agree to a certain extent. I think people have to know what's possible.
70 I think they have to know what they don't know in the sense that I don't think that reporters
71 can really do their jobs if they continue to do it or just did it in the same way say five or ten
72 years ago. Because there are new ways to do reporting and there are new tools that help you
73 do reporting in a changing environment. But I think, you know, Simon's right in the sense
74 that it's a bad thing for journalists to be ignorant about working with data. I think, you know,
75 there are a lot of risks there, one of them is that you're not going to get good stories, you
76 know, you're going to miss some stories, you're just not going to be able to do them. And
77 then the other one is that you're going to be beaten by people who can and that's not a good
78 thing, obviously. Not only, you know, for the individual journalist, but for the industry as a
79 whole for us to sort of, you know, for everyone to be able to say: "I don't really need this."
80 You know, I think that's kind of a mistake. I would say there's one caveat to that, if you can
81 write, you know, really well, like, you write like Tolstoi, you should just spend all of your
82 time writing. Any time that you don't spend writing is a misuse of your time. But for most of
83 us, you know, I can't write like that, I'm not that good of a writer, for most of us it's
84 important to at least know, what's possible and to know, sort of, what the people and the
85 organizations and the institutions that you cover, how they're using data and so you'll have
86 some way to sort of evaluate what they do.

87 F: Okay, so you've mentioned before that the world is increasingly made up of data,
88 everybody's gathering data or we produce data as we walk through our day. So if you would

89   sum up, what are the perks of data journalism in this perspective, what would lure someone to
90   data journalism who was a traditional journalist before?

91   // 00:10:42

92   A: A couple of things. I think one is the ability to do definitive stories. I think that's really sort
93   of compelling because you can really say: "Now I either proved or disproved this theory I had
94   and there's something pretty satisfying about that. The other thing is that it's in demand. I
95   mean there are people who're valuate and you know, we're not, this industry is not, you
96   know, we have our issues with making money, with people being able to keep their jobs and I
97   would think, like, on a solely on a sort of selfish, self-preservation basis it would not be a bad
98   way to go, if it doesn't intrusively interest you. But I think the other thing is that, you know,
99   and the thing that I hope would appeal to almost any journalist is that it gives you, it can give
100   you the tools to answer and address really interesting questions that otherwise you might think
101   are beyond your means to do. And I think if we're going to really sort of thrive as an industry
102   we have to be able to, and eager to answer and to tackle and answer really interesting
103   questions. Otherwise I'm not sure why readers would stick with us. So I think the fact that it
104   can make you not only a better reporter but a reporter who's better able to address really
105   interesting stuff, you know, to me, that's incentive enough.

106   F: Okay, there's this side of the medal but of course there's the downsides of data journalism
107   like sources. The sources of data. So if you take a respectable source as a given, so you don't
108   have to care about that problem anymore, is there a potential new kind of truth in massively
109   gathered data that journalists should and have to report about? Is there this new aspect of
110   reality maybe that you have to report about as a journalist?

111   // 00:12:57

112   A: Yeah, I think there is. But you also have to be sort of very careful about, you know, when
113   you're dealing with data and you think that it represents something that it doesn't, both in
114   terms of what the data is actually saying and maybe how it was gathered and collected but
115   also like where that data is coming from and who are the sort of original sources of it. A great
116   example is something like Twitter, which we love. People love to see things like maps based
117   on, you know tweets based on, you know, World Cup fans and you know, teams and players
118   and they can be very interesting and telling in some circumstances. But I think what we have
119   to keep in mind when we work with any dataset is that it may not represent the entirety of the
120   population of the world, you know. It may not represent the people that you, all the people

121 that you're wanting to describe, you know we have to be really careful about how we source
122 things and how we describe things and we have to be very careful not to sort of assume that
123 everybody sees whatever data we're working with in the exact same way that we do. Because
124 if you work with data long enough, you start to feel that you know it, and you and the data are
125 understanding each other and, you know, translating that to, and then just putting it in front of
126 other people, you know, they're not going to have the same understanding or approach it the
127 same way you do and I think you have to be really, really careful about you know, sort of, the
128 same way that you would background the people that you're interviewing or the organizations
129 that you're reporting on, you have to background your data, you have to know where it comes
130 from, know what it represents and what it doesn't represent. And I think one of the biggest
131 issues we have, just in general, is that we, when we get a dataset, very rarely do we start out
132 thinking: "What's not in here?" Because, you know, you're spending your time looking for
133 what is in the dataset, but you're not really thinking: "What isn't there?"

134 F: The blind spots.

135 // 00:15:20

136 A: Right, and very often that can be a really, really crucial information in itself.

137 F: Okay. Is there some sort of reflection of the sources and the biases which are in data which
138 actually come popping up in the articles about it? Is there some reflection that you actually
139 give back to the public with it, which would be necessary maybe?

140 // 00:15:48

141 A: Yeah, I think oftentimes it is very necessary. It's something that's a little awkward
142 sometimes because it's not something that journalists are really used to doing. But I do think
143 that it's important to like, for example to say what you don't know or what the data doesn't,
144 isn't able to tell you because, again, like I think with a lot of people, whether they're
145 journalists or not, the implication of that "I have a dataset, it's going to answer all of my
146 questions, it's going to solve my problems. There's few datasets that will actually do that.
147 You know, when you're writing about data it is very important to sort be able to be honest
148 with the readers and say: "Look, this doesn't answer every question here or it may not even
149 fully answer the question I'm interested in. What it can do, you know, is serve as a proxy for
150 that question." And to ensure that readers know that, I think it's, that's on us to do. Because,

151 otherwise, you live under the production that it's a little more certain than you think it is. And
152 that's a bad position to be in.

153 F: But is that the practice yet? That you really make clear in the articles and in the stuff you
154 publish based on the data that there may be blind spots and there's always this certain
155 perspective you can portray but not everything?

156 // 00:17:21

157 A: I think… I don't know if it's sort as ingrained as other practices but I do see it more often,
158 especially among organizations and journalists who use data a lot. Because everybody will
159 make a mistake or everyone will get something slightly wrong or, you know, more than
160 slightly wrong and that are the chasings that will sort of remind you, you know, I really can't
161 go out this far on a limp and not acknowledge the weaknesses and vulnerabilities here, so I
162 think that the folks that are, the outlets that are really good at using data, treated as a sort of
163 state of the art of the reporting process, they know this. Sometimes, you know, what we used
164 to do, years ago, and I still see this occasionally, is that you put like a little box next to a story
165 that describes the methodology and some weaknesses. And I think that's okay but honestly I
166 think the better part is to put it right in the story and say: "Look, here's what we don't know
167 about this. Here's the weakness of this data." Or: "Here's the flaw, the potential flaw that
168 might have, that makes us a little less confident." And I think the more that we do that, as
169 uncomfortable and unnatural it might seem at first, I think the better off everybody is going to
170 be.

171 F: Of course, but it's a point of selling your story, too. If you put emphasis on the weaknesses
172 maybe you can't have so many units sold or so many clicks gathered.

173 // 00:18:59

174 A: Right, I think there's definitely this tension about like: "Well, we want to have a good
175 story." Well, I mean, I think we sort of have to realize that our readers, if they want to, on the
176 internet, can kind of follow our tracks a little bit, you know, they can usually find the source
177 of the data or find out what other people are saying about it. And so in most cases, if you
178 don't acknowledge that stuff, you're going to be found out at some point. And so I think it's
179 the better part, it's the right thing to do for us to acknowledge it as upfront as we can.

180 F: So, to the upsides of data journalism, is there a new sort of legitimacy that journalists can
181 add to their claims using data? You've mentioned some sort of that before, but how about
182 legitimacy?

183 // 00:19:59

184 A: Yeah, I think so, I mean you have to be really careful about, you know, sort of, saying that
185 it's kind of an holy grail or anything. It's only really as good as, obviously, the people who
186 create the data and whatever we do to interpret it. But I do think that there is a really
187 important thing that we can take away from using data, I mean, we can actually get closer to
188 certainty, we can actually say: "Look, this isn't just us interviewing a couple of people and
189 telling you what they think." This is really what these patterns look like over time or this is
190 really what some other information in the data would suggest you as well. I think that's a
191 good thing, I think that the issues usually come from us sort of maybe trying to, you know,
192 sell a little bit too much or rely on only that. I mean, like I said, I interview data but I can't
193 just interview data. I have to talk to people, I have to read other things. You know, in almost
194 every case the data alone isn't going to tell you everything that I need and I think that's the
195 other aspect at play here that the people have to, that the journalists have to consider is that,
196 it's a great tool, but it can't be, it shouldn't be your only tool.

197 F: Okay. But that specific tool, which sometimes incorporates, like, scientific methods, is it
198 capable of bringing some kind of new objectivity to the table? To journalistic claims or like
199 an article that is written from some sort of perspective is going into an objective kind of
200 direction instead of being like a subjective piece?

201 // 00:22:03

202 A: I think we have to be very careful about, sort of, I mean what I, very few of us, at least in
203 journalism that now work with data, are doing social science. Some of our methods are the
204 same or similar, but, you know, compared to, you know, your average economist or
205 behavioral scientist, we're not doing a lot of that. You know, the most that we, the furthest
206 that we get into that stuff is, like, regression analysis and maybe some other types of
207 modeling, some basic modeling types of things. But I think we have to be really careful about
208 what we're not trying to do here which is we're not really trying to establish per se, we're
209 trying to find out, basically, what happened. And that's... You know, those two are similar
210 and sometimes overlap but I think we have to be careful not to sort of get carried away with,
211 sort of, the belief like "Oh, because I'm working with data, therefore I get to, you know, I'm

212   now sort of Superman and I now make pronunciations from the mountaintop and I deliver the
213   truth." You know, I think it's people might start out with that and they might think after a
214   couple of stories they're like "Oh, this is really powerful and it gives me a much better
215   platform." But eventually, I think, they're probably going to find out that it's not as powerful
216   as they think it is and that there are a lot of other things involved in that. So I think it's, you
217   know, I think it's complicated, it's not a cut-and-dry thing. I would love to say: "Yeah, the
218   New York Times is now five percent more objective than it were." But I don't even know
219   how to measure that and I'm not sure I would want us to start shooting for the pursuit of
220   scientific truths in some respects.

221   F: Yeah, that's very interesting. Have you already witnessed some data journalists finding
222   their revelation, that data is not the truth and not capable of putting them on the
223   mountaintops? Has there been some "falling"?

224   // 00:24:28

225   A: Yeah, I mean, a lot of the times, a lot of the mistakes the folks make and I include myself
226   in this, is that you presume things, that aren't, you know, that's not the case. You don't
227   understand the data well enough to make the right interpretation. But the other part is that,
228   like... Or you just make simple mistakes, like mathematical errors and calculation errors and
229   those can happen. So that's a simple way of reminding you that you aren't as smart as you
230   were or you still have a lot to learn. You know, I think it's not that different overall from other
231   parts of reporting, where you also make mistakes or you get names wrong or you get dates
232   wrong or you get a fact wrong somewhere and, you know, I think they're roughly equivalent
233   in the sense that they're both things you're trying to avoid but, being human, we'll still do
234   from time to time. I do think that, like, it can seem for some folks, the fact that a computer
235   spits out some number, can seem more authoritative than it otherwise should be and they have
236   this sort of trust in the computer that usually comes from the sense of "Well, the computer
237   seems smarter than I am." Which might be true somewhere down the road but it's not true
238   now and any analysis you're doing with data using a computer is only as good as you really
239   are and is only as good as your understanding of the data. So I think it's important to sort of...
240   Yeah, I mean, we're all are going to make mistakes, we all do mistakes and I think the
241   important thing to do is to not give a computer, you know, more credit than it deserves, more
242   respect that it deserves and to be really skeptical about what we know and what we think we
243   know. The same way we would if somebody were telling us a story and we were writing it
244   down and be like "Ah, maybe I should check this out."

245   F: Yeah, okay, so on the perks side of data journalism we already mentioned the blind spots of
246   reporting, do you think that in a world that is increasingly documented in data, can data
247   journalists broaden the range of picturing the reality? Is there some kind of potential to be
248   more complete?

249   *// 00:27:07*

250   A: I think so, I think that's absolutely one of the biggest strengths of it or potential strengths is
251   that our ability to sort of describe and what goes on in it is limited by a bunch of things. It is
252   limited by our ability to be in certain places at certain times. It's limited by our ability to be,
253   our need for sleep and to eat and to be able to talk to our friends and family. And computers
254   don't have those needs. And so… For example, one of the things I work with a lot is political
255   fundraising data and the reports about what people raise and spend on campaigns they're filed
256   on a pretty much around the clock basis. Not all day, every day, but they come in at all hours
257   of the day and night and there is no way that I personally could sit and watch them come in
258   and look at each one and decide what's interesting or potentially newsworthy. But I can have
259   a computer do that for me. And so that's what I do, I have a computer tell me: "Oh hey, this
260   one looks interesting because you told me to look out for these particular factors or this type
261   of situation." And when you have that sort of approach, it enables me to, you know, I'm not
262   looking at every filing, but in a way I am. It enables me to do things I otherwise couldn't do.
263   Similarly, if you're talking about describing, you know, say, we did this during the World
264   Cup, where you get data, you know, folks have cameras all around the stadium and they will
265   tell you, like, who touches the ball when and for how long, who controls the ball and then
266   passes the ball. And image if you were a human trying to sort of write that down on the fly,
267   it's crazy! But we can get it, thanks to cameras and computers that don't have to worry about
268   taking breaks or, you know, getting distracted by something and so I think it does give us the
269   possibility that we can do things that we would not otherwise be able to do. And that's a huge
270   benefit, that's just an enormous benefit of it. I think the equivalent is to say, like, well, I could
271   dip a glass into the river and take out a glass, a cup of water, or I could just basically, take out
272   almost all of the river on an ongoing… You know, I mean it's what you miss by doing just a
273   glass full can be pretty important and so I think to the extent that we have the ability to
274   actually expand our scope because of using data, we should take advantage of it.

275   F: Okay, but the distinction of what is relevant for your reporting cannot be done by a
276   computer. That is an ability that is a journalist's professional thing. So do data journalists
277   have to be programming geeks so to speak in order to make programs see the world in their

278   own view in regard of relevance and stuff? Do they have to program their own things to make
279   sure the programs record the right thing, the right river if you will?

280   // 00:31:03

281   A: Right, I think it's, yeah, and that's the new and hard part. It's to try to teach the computer
282   to model the slice of real life that you're looking at or to be some kind of stand-in in some
283   respects. So I think, you know, that is sort of the thing that makes data journalism interesting.
284   It's not the fact that computers can do things on a, you know, on an automated basis and
285   quickly – it's the fact that you can bring the journalistic sort of knowledge and sensibility and
286   combine that with what a computer can do and then you get a much better sort of output. I
287   think the hard part is really sort of getting... I mean it's funny, because it's like we approach
288   this from two ways. One is we take journalists and we try to sort of convert them into data
289   people, to make working with data part of their routine. And that's pretty hard in a lot of
290   respects. But sometimes it's easier to do that than it is to take people who are computer
291   scientists or developers and teach them what journalists do and what they think about because
292   it's such an odd profession, it's just a non-standard kind of thing. I tell engineers about, like,
293   the process of journalism and they're horrified by how inefficient it is and it just seems sort of
294   random. And so we try to... We've done both of it at the Times, you know, we have people
295   who we've hired were developed from within journalism, from within the Times to work with
296   data and then we've hired people from outside of journalism and we can teach them, you
297   know, we try to teach them a lot about sort of how a newsroom works and how journalists
298   work and think and hope that it clicks at some point. But that's the other thing that makes us
299   different from social scientists or data scientists, it's that... I see a lot of, I go to a lot of
300   conferences and I see a lot of, you know, at academic conferences in particular, I see a lot of
301   projects that are using really interesting, let's say, really interesting algorithm, but you're
302   using it on a dataset that I couldn't care anything about and I would be like "Wow, that's
303   really interesting if it were applied to something that, like, people really care about, that
304   would be really amazing." And I think that's what we should be doing more of. It's just sort
305   of "Okay, what are their great approaches and tools and techniques out there" and then "Let's
306   apply them to the things that, as journalists, we are reasonably certain the public cares about
307   or will care about once we do it."

308   F: Okay, so it's a hard thing to bring traditional journalists to using data. Are there any data
309   journalists who are some sort of less geeky and still use those data journalism tools someone

310 else develops, is there such a thing? Like a not-really-a-hacker journalist that just uses some
311 Python code or something like that?

312 *// 00:34:31*

313 A: It actually goes even, it starts even earlier in the sense of you people, you know, we
314 journalists are very good at Excel, like, they are great at spreadsheets and they're probably not
315 ever going beyond spreadsheets. But they are great at spreadsheets. And if you're pretty good
316 at spreadsheets you can still do quite a lot of stuff. And there's a whole wide range of people
317 in terms of other skills and the tools that they use. You know, I tell people in trainings "All
318 you ever do is get reasonably good at Excel or Google Spreadsheets, you're going to be ahead
319 of most working journalists in terms of your technical abilities. You're going to have an
320 advantage, even just with that. And so there's a whole range of... You don't have to go the
321 full-on programming or data science stuff or using R or... You can kind of choose at what
322 point you feel most comfortable and stick with that. I think, actually, if more people did that,
323 I'd be thrilled.

324 F: Okay, but still: Is there maybe those lazy people in the business who want to keep up with
325 data journalism and just trust the tools others program for them? Is there maybe some people
326 who ride the bus for free? There's a word for it...

327 *// 00:36:05*

328 A: Yeah, I mean, there's a long tradition of that. Of sort of asking experts "Hey, what do you
329 guys think or what does your analysis say and we're going to write that up." I don't want to
330 say that that's not legitimate, I think it's totally legitimate in some cases. In many cases. I
331 think where we can either build on it or replicate it or do something totally new on something,
332 we should. We should try to do that. But where it's something that frankly is interesting on its
333 own, a replication would be, you know, wouldn't really advance the ball that much. I don't
334 have a problem with that sort of thing. I do think, what I do have a problem is where, is where
335 reporters would say "Well, what they do is something I could never even approach." I mean, I
336 think, maybe yes, but you should really find out. You know?

337 F: Okay, let's talk about the reflection the data journalistic methods again. We mentioned it
338 before, but there seems to be lacking a discourse of methods maybe inside those articles. In
339 what way do data journalists day by day reflect their methods, would you say, which is not,
340 you know, coming out of those articles?

341 // 00:37:43

342 A: Yeah, there's been a lot of discussion about this for a long time. About what do we have,
343 how much do we tell our readers about what it is that we're doing exactly. You know, I can
344 see, it's still not exactly an unresolved thing because I think there are... You know, I think
345 there are some good points in the sense of, like, "Well, do really want to put every last thing
346 we do in front of..." Not only in concern of, like, this is going to be a, because it'll be a, you
347 know, because we are embarrassed to do it, but how much does a reader need to know, to sort
348 of get the point and understand what we are talking about. How much do we need, and to
349 what extend should we then provide them with the means or the materials to sort of go deeper.
350 When the internet wasn't really involved, this was an easy question. Editors just said: "Look,
351 we don't have the space, we're not going to bore readers with this stuff. So forget it." But
352 we've been online for long enough now, to sort of, you know, to have a much better
353 conversation and get to a slightly better place on this question and I don't really think that we
354 have done that. I think we try to where it's sort of appropriate, we try to make or underlying
355 data available. I think we have gotten better about explaining methodology, about the
356 particular approaches we're taking in many cases. But I do thing that there is still, between the
357 sort of combination of "I don't want to bore readers" and "I don't want to give away, sort of,
358 potentially competitive information with a purchase." Between those two factors I think
359 there's a lot of, you know, there's still, it's not quite, we haven't really found exactly the right
360 place for it. I mean, I think in most cases, like, readers are not stupid and telling them things is
361 not a bad way to go. It's just that it think there's a, there's really long being like "Well, is that
362 really what readers want from us." I think, you know, I think as we get a sort of more
363 sophisticated web audience, I think we're going to have to figure this out, find out a way to do
364 this, that doesn't insult their intelligence and also makes us feel we're doing the right thing
365 and comfortable all the rest of it.

366 F: So do you think that's a probable future scenario that the readers will choose the
367 publication with the best or the most transparent methodology? Is that a selling point maybe?

368 // 00:40:46

369 A: I mean, it certainly could be and some readers will gravitate towards that. I don't know
370 how many, but some will. But I think, you know, it'll be easier for people to be able to sort of
371 judge us when we do this. And I that's only going to help in the sense that, you know, we're
372 getting to the point now where it's, you know, people are already there, people are already

373 able to, kind of, to switch around from this source to that source. And I think, like, to the
374 extent that we, if they don't really know us or aren't really familiar with us, to the extent that
375 we can reassure them "Hey look, this is how we do things here." Then that's probably the
376 better thing to do.

377 F: Okay, what are maybe the things that keep data journalists from giving transparency to
378 their methodology, is it time or is it maybe the lack of motivation to write about all the stuff
379 that you've done and not the story itself, what would you say?

380 // 00:42:02

381 A: I think most of it is, some of it might be a little bit of time, but a lot of it goes down to,
382 they find the story more interesting than the methodology. And they think readers find stories
383 more interesting than the methodology and I hope most readers do. But I would say, we
384 should probably figure out a way to do both. You know, without really sort of, you know,
385 without sort of compromising both.

386 F: Okay, that's about it with my questions, I thank you a lot. […]

387 // 00:42:38